BERTRAND RUSSELL'S ETHICS

Continuum Studies in British Philosophy:
Series Editor: James Fieser, University of Tennessee at Martin

Duncan Richter, *Wittgenstein at his Word*
Wilfrid E. Rumble, *Doing Austin Justice*
María J. Frápolli (ed.), *F. P. Ramsey: Critical Reassessments*
William R. Eaton, *Boyle on Fire*
David Berman, *Berkeley and Irish Philosophy*
Colin Tyler, *Radical Philosophy*
Stephen Lalor, *Matthew Tindal, Freethinker: An 18th-century assault on religion*
Michael K. Potter, *Bertrand Russell's Ethics*
Angela M. Coventry, *Hume's Theory of Causation*
Colin Heydt, *Rethinking Mill's Ethics*
Stephen J. Finn, *Thomas Hobbes and The Politics of Natural Philosophy*
John R. Fitzpatrick, *John Stuart Mill's Political Philosophy*
J. Mark Lazenby, *The Early Wittgenstein on Religion*
Dennis Desroches, *Francis Bacon and the Limits of Scientific Knowledge*
Megan Laverty, *Iris Murdoch's Ethics*
William C. Davis, *Thomas Reid's Ethics*
John H. Sceski, *Popper, Objectivity and the Growth of Knowledge*
Talia Mae Bettcher, *Berkeley's Philosophy of Spirit*
Eric Brandon, *The Coherence of Hobbes's* Leviathan
Patricia Sheridan, *Locke's Moral Theory*
J. Jeremy Wisnewski, *Wittgenstein and Ethical Inquiry*
Rosalind Carey, *Russell and Wittgenstein on the Nature of Judgement*
Michael Taylor, *The Philosophy of Herbert Spencer*
James E. Crimmins, *Jeremy Bentham's Final Years*
James G. Buickerood, *John Locke on Imagination and the Passions*

Bertrand Russell's Ethics

MICHAEL K. POTTER

continuum
LONDON • NEW YORK

Continuum
The Tower Building
11 York Road
London SE1 7NX

15 East 26th Street
New York
NY 10010

British Library Cataloguing-in-Publication Data
A catalogue record for this book is available from the British Library.

ISBN: HB: 0-8264-8810-2

Typeset by YHT Ltd, London
Printed and bound in Great Britain by MPG Books Ltd, Bodmin, Cornwall

CONTENTS

Acknowledgements   ix
Preface   xi

1 Descent Into Emotivism   1
2 A Critique of Basic Emotivism   18
3 Enlightened Emotivism   82
4 Impulse and Desire   123
5 Final Thoughts   159

Bibliography   176
Index   183

To Phil Gosselin, May Yoh, and Steve Robinson for getting me into this mess, encouraging me to continue, challenging me, arguing, and discussing. I'm a better person for having known you.

ACKNOWLEDGEMENTS

Completion of this project was a long, hard journey. It began as an MA thesis in the department of philosophy at McMaster University. Due to all sorts of troubles, primarily health related, the project stalled several times, hit a few dead ends, and was eventually submitted several months late. I owe my supervisory committee – Nicholas Griffin, Kenneth Blackwell, and Sami Najm – tremendous gratitude for their patience. Each of them made innumerable helpful suggestions, comments and criticisms, coming up with possibilities I would not have otherwise considered. The reader will find their names strewn throughout the endnotes. Nick Griffin, especially, was instrumental in helping me shape this project in its last few months.

I'd like to acknowledge my family for supporting me in a variety of ways, sometimes against my will! Special thanks to Karin and Kieran Potter, Barry and Lois Dickson, Alison and Luc Simard, Harry and Susan Wiens, and Robert Potter.

My colleagues at McMaster University have broadened my horizons and provided much-needed relaxing conversation. Most significantly, thanks to Saul Geniusas for confusing me with his bizarre alien philosophies, forcing me to think about issues in ways I'd never have otherwise considered. McMaster University itself also deserves credit for its financial support, work space and interesting classes.

Thanks to May Yoh for stirring up my interest in Russell, and for creating a course on Russell while I was an undergraduate at Brandon University. This book would never have come to be without her early encouragement.

Thanks to Charles Pigden for renewing interest in Russell's ethics, and for his ideas – of which I have made liberal use.

And, finally, I cannot forget to thank Philip de Bary at Continuum, who had the remarkably good taste to move forward with this book!

That's all.

PREFACE

Bertrand Russell was not only one of the greatest philosophers of the twentieth century, he was also a humanitarian activist who fought for a variety of moral, social and political causes. During his lifetime, the general public knew him for his activism and popular works, in which he tackled such diverse topics as sexual ethics, religion, war and nuclear disarmament. The philosophical world, on the other hand, knew him for his work in mathematical logic and philosophy of mathematics.

Unbeknownst to most people in both groups, Russell was a pioneer in moral philosophy, and his work in that area not only informed and guided his activism, it contained some genuinely groundbreaking ideas. Russell created one of the first versions of a metaethical theory known as emotivism – later briefly popularized by A.J. Ayer and C.L. Stevenson – which maintains that moral utterances cannot be true or false, just expressions of a wish, desire or attitude. Yet, despite the fact that Russell held on to some form of emotivism for most of his professional life, and despite the fact that the theory is present in some of his best-known books, it was virtually ignored until Charles Pigden published *Russell on Ethics* – a collection of Russell's ethical essays and excerpts – in 1998.

Some have questioned the apparent inconsistency between emotivism and activism. Isn't an activist moved by the conviction that his moral beliefs are true? We will discover that Russell's enlightened emotivism makes room for activism and strong moral feeling. He understood the importance of practical application in all branches of moral philosophy, and that the ultimate purpose of moral philosophy is to help human beings live better lives. That Russell could hold an emotivist theory while being, at the same time, an ardent activist is quite a feat. That his version was vastly superior to more popular versions of emotivism is another.

In this book we will take a comprehensive and critical look at Russell's emotivism. The reader is invited to join in a serious critical investigation of Russell's ethical theorizing, and thus come to a better understanding of his life, activism and contribution to moral philosophy.

We begin, in Chapter 1, with a discussion of the reasons behind Russell's development of his emotivism just prior to and during the First World War. Because Russell turned to emotivism while also stepping up his activism, the genesis and development of his metaethic needs to be contextualized. Russell's philosophy was often influenced by events in the world, and his metaethic was no exception. It was in part a consequence of, and a reaction against, personal and political events that had a dramatic impact on his life.

In Chapter 2, we examine the more popular emotivisms of A.J. Ayer and C.L. Stevenson, comparing them to Russell's early 'proto-emotivism' – an underdeveloped mishmash of subjectivist and emotivist ideas. Ayer and Stevenson see their theories fall to several objections, though Stevenson's, at least, is stronger than popularly assumed. Russell's proto-emotivism, since it is barely a theory at all, is also a failure. Nevertheless, it lays the groundwork for what is to come.

In Chapter 3, we trace the development of Russell's emotivism into a more refined and mature 'enlightened emotivism'. By contrasting Russell's emotivism with the rival theories of Ayer and Stevenson, we find that Russell's enlightened emotivism is able to meet or avoid most of the problems that cripple its rivals, is better able to fulfill the purposes of a metaethical theory, and informs his normative ethics and activism.

Of the problems that remain, many can be resolved by incorporating Russell's much-overlooked philosophical psychology (his theories of desire and impulse) – from *The Analysis of Mind* and *Principles of Social Reconstruction* – into his emotivist metaethic. Although Russell alludes to this work in his moral philosophy, he doesn't actually pursue the connection – nor has anyone else in the decades since. In chapter four, then, we perform the synthesis on his behalf, and the result is a much more sophisticated theory, perhaps the most compelling variety of emotivism to be found in twentieth-century philosophy.

Finally, in Chapter 5, we consider some strategies for strengthening Russell's theory further, and consider what it means for moral philosophy today. If in the end it is not persuasive, it still provides useful insights into the nature of ethical thought and behaviour that anyone interested in ethics ought to take seriously. And to the extent that Russell succeeds where Ayer and Stevenson failed, we ought to conclude that emotivism deserves more respect than it presently receives.

Although metaethics is sometimes characterized as the more 'technical' and 'obscure' branch of ethics, the present work is intended to be accessible to the intelligent layperson, as well as useful to philosophers and other scholars. Jargon is explained and a minimum number of assumptions are made about the reader's knowledge of philosophy.

1

Descent Into Emotivism

Emotivism is now considered the Kentucky cousin of moral philosophy. Once a promising new approach to the understanding of ethical language, it has become a curiosity, an intriguing blemish, in the history of twentieth-century ethics. Nevertheless, though few contemporary philosophers are inclined to sully their names with the emotivist label, while it reigned this theory caught the attention of several philosophical heavyweights, the best known of whom are A.J. Ayer and C.L. Stevenson.

Bertrand Russell is a vastly more important figure in twentieth-century philosophy than both Ayer and Stevenson, but most do not associate his name with emotivism – or indeed with moral philosophy at all. Nonetheless, not only did Russell advance an early form of emotivism before Ayer and Stevenson felt the urge, his refined theory is more plausible, more complete, and less vulnerable to attack than its better-known rivals. Despite the fact that it ultimately fails as a metaethical theory, there is much that we can learn from it. Indeed, the insights Russell's emotivist metaethic provides could inform approaches to metaethics even now. In the pages to come, we will examine the emotivist theories of Ayer and Stevenson, setting them against Russell's emotivism in both its early and refined forms. We will discover that Russell's early emotivism falls prey to many of the same criticisms that cripple its more popular rivals. Yet we will also find that Russell's refined emotivist theory – his 'enlightened emotivism' – manages to overcome many of the obstacles faced by the others by taking advantage of the insights provided by his theories of desire and impulse, resulting in a construct distinctly superior to those of Ayer and Stevenson in every significant way. In the end, however, though it may be a superior sort of emotivism, this may not prevent Russell's enlightened emotivism from being an insufficient metaethic.

But there is more to consider than simply how Russell's emotivism stacks up against other varieties. Although little serious attention has been paid to Russell's moral philosophy, a great deal has been paid to his moral activism – activism for a range of social and political causes, stretching from just before the First World War to his death. He is, in other words, recognized as an active moralist, if not a moral philosopher, someone committed to persuading others to share his moral opinions. Just as he began to commit serious time to activism, Russell began to turn toward emotivism, which denies that moral propositions can have any truth-value at all. That an individual could promote a pacifist cause while denying that the proposition 'War is morally wrong' is capable of being true or false may strike some as absurd. We will come to see, however, that one of the insights provided by Russell's enlightened emotivism is that there is no necessary absurdity or hypocrisy in the coexistence of emotivism and activism.

The Prig Before the Storm

The period during which Russell dived into emotivism (and activism) was one of the most tumultuous of his life – and we cannot understand the changes in Russell's intellectual and political lives unless we understand the context in which they occurred. We are faced with a man who, *prior* to 1914, was 'a slightly priggish academic creature, keeping brilliant company, thinking brilliant thoughts and writing brilliant books on mathematics and philosophy',[1] showing, much of the time, little more than intellectual curiosity for moral issues in the public sphere. We are faced with a man who, *from* about 1914, pursued his moral causes as though led by the hand of God and in doing so alienated many of his friends and colleagues – all the while leaning toward a metaethic that denied the very possibility of moral truth.

The Russell of the pre-war world was committed to Moorean intuitionism, an absolutist metaethic centred on the claim that specifically moral, non-natural, qualities of goodness and bad-ness must exist if moral judgments are to be capable of truth and falsity – unless, that is, moral concepts and judgments can be reduced to *non*-moral concepts and judgments. If such non-natural qualities exist, they will not be accessible to our senses; our only access to them would be through 'intuition'.[2]

Although it may not be obvious, Russell's allegiance to Moorean intuitionism was actually a step up from his previous theory: a naive yet intriguing form of simple subjectivism, a 'desire to desire' theory of ethics.[3] In it, 'X is good' meant nothing more than 'I desire to desire X', a statement that one has a certain psychological state, leaving ethics as a somewhat trivial branch of psychology. Fortunately for Russell, he did not hold on to this theory for very long. And, fortunately for his development as an emotivist, he returned to the glimmerings of insight found in this early theory when refining his enlightened emotivism in the 1920s and '30s.

Eventually, Russell grew out of intuitionism. As he described it:

The period from 1910 to 1914 was a time of transition. . . . I underwent a process of rejuvenation, inaugurated by Ottoline Morrell and continued by the War. It may seem curious that the War should rejuvenate anybody, but in fact it shook me out of my prejudices and made me think afresh on a number of fundamental questions. It also provided me with a new kind of activity [political activism], for which I did not feel the

staleness that beset me whenever I tried to return to mathematical logic.[4]

There was, of course, no magic moment, no point at which
something clicked and Russell became a changed man. Doubts
appear to have begun as a consequence of his theory of
descriptions, which could not be reconciled with intuitionism.

Late in life, Russell wrote that George Santayana's mockery of
Moorean intuitionism, in *Winds of Doctrine* (1913), caused him to
abandon his belief in the objectivity of good and evil, for if there
could be no property of goodness, as Santayana claimed, and
thus no true primary ascriptions of goodness to objects (as the
theory of descriptions had already indicated on entirely independent grounds), then nothing could be good. Santayana
believed that ethical absolutism was an illusion borne of malevolence, and that abandoning such nonsense would lead to
greater tolerance and understanding. Presumably, he thought
tolerance and understanding were good – absolutely? In time,
Russell 'came to agree, both about the non-existence of an
objective good and about the beneficial effects if this doctrine
were widely believed'.[5] He must have been plagued by doubt
already, or he would have laughed off Santayana's vicious ridicule – and it *is* merely ridicule; Santayana does not bother to
argue for his condemnation of objective ethics.[6] In fact, Russell
did say that at first he wasn't convinced by Santayana's criticisms;
whatever role they played, they were insufficient to change his
mind on their own.[7]

Harry Ruja claims that Russell changed readily into an emotivist because he had never actually been a committed Moorean[8]
– his 'desire to desire' theory (or, at least, his conviction of the
primacy of desire in ethics) was always lurking in the background. Ruja suggests that Russell's 'desire to desire' theory
presented him with such problems 'that he turned to Moore's
simplistic doctrine to escape those problems. But when

Santayana poked fun at the hypostatized good, Russell was glad to desert it and he returned to the relativity of good to desire' – and thus had little interest in defending himself against Santayana's attack.[9] Clearly, Russell had always quarrelled with Moore on specific points, and certainly, as Ruja claims, 'the period of Russell's discipleship in ethics to Moore was but an interlude between Russell's early and late periods during both of which he was loyal to the principle of the relativity of good to desire'.[10] But to characterize this as the entire, or nearly entire, story ignores the significant impact that the aforementioned difficulties, not to mention events outside of philosophy, had on Russell's life and mind. Additionally, to characterize Russell as one who simply needed a prod to embrace emotivism ignores the obvious discomfort Russell felt as an emotivist. During his prolonged intellectual commitment to emotivism, Russell at least *claimed* that he desired objective ethics, that he wanted to believe in the truth and falsity of ethical propositions. We have no reason to doubt him.

But is it true that Russell was not a committed Moorean? Apparently not. Yes, he did have a barely suppressed commitment to, or preoccupation with, the role of desire in the back of his mind at all times, and yes, he had never been an orthodox Moorean; but he was emotionally committed to belief in objective good and evil, and intellectually to the general features of Moore's intuitionism.

One crucial factor in Russell's switch to emotivism may have been a result of his admirable commitment to putting theory into practice. While an intuitionist, he attempted to practice what he preached, and it led to appalling consequences – intuitionism played a large role in the dissolution of his marriage to his first wife, Alys, and his unwillingness to seek a divorce for many years. The austerity of Moorean ethics, its contention that the Good has nothing to do with human beings and their needs, led to an emotionless, robotic sort of life.[11] Thus, Russell was well aware of the consequences of this 'objective' position and was searching for an alternative conception. His disastrous application of Moorean intuitionism may also have led him to realize that it lacked a reliable intellectual foundation, as many subsequent moral philosophers have argued.

Regardless, Santayana's book does not appear to have changed Russell's mind immediately. A more likely consequence is that it led him into further doubt. Although he read *Winds of Doctrine* in 1913, Russell did not explicitly take his baby steps toward emotivism until the following year. Even then, as Pigden writes, 'Russell's arguments for his view . . . are not so much arguments *for* proto-emotivism as *against* the Moorean good'.[12] Though he may have been led to doubt moral objectivity, he may not have embraced emotivism *per se* during this period, but rather a form of simple subjectivism containing emotivist elements – elements that gradually overtook the theory during the First World War.

With all due respect to Santayana's devastating wit, other factors played a larger role in Russell's conversion.

A Woman and a War

Russell's relationship with Ottoline Morrell changed his life in several different ways; in the words of the more reliable of his biographers: 'The First World War was to create the decisive watershed in Russell's life. Ottoline prepared him for it.'[13] The character and quality of their relationship fluctuated over the years, and at several points it nearly imploded. It was an affair of desperate longing and admiration on Russell's part – and a mixture of fascination, love and ambivalence on Ottoline's. In Ottoline, Russell saw an intoxicating combination of muse, lover and confidante. She was his inspiration, a dazzling, romantic and worldly woman who could not bring herself to commit totally to him, for she had no wish to abandon her husband and daughter. In a 1914 letter to her, Russell attempted to explain the difference she had made in his life. Whitehead, he wrote, had noticed significant changes in him: 'He says I used to have great ingenuity in defending rather narrow & limited points of view, but now I have an altogether broader scope . . . I think it is true, & it is really largely due to you.'[14]

Because of Ottoline, Russell's interests – which were never as narrow as Russell himself believed – became even broader, his character more understanding and tolerant. He lost the austerity and priggishness of his youth and became something far more human, a man whose emotions were given licence to present themselves, who no longer kept his passions bottled up inside. He even believed that Ottoline helped him develop a greater appreciation of art, literature and music. When Russell became involved with her in 1911, he was in the midst of a crippling depression, brought about in part by the deterioration of his marriage to Alys Pearsall-Smith. Ottoline struck him as a sort of saviour – a kind, passionate, peaceful woman possessed of vast insight and virtue. Clearly, Russell idealized her; still, he was correct about her impact on his life.

Though he was devoted to Ottoline for decades, and would have sold his soul to please her, religious differences prevented them from fully realizing the potential of their relationship. She accepted without question much of the religion that had been drilled into her as a girl (in a vague, non-doctrinal sense), but this 'was set against a background of mystic wonder at natural beauty; at the inexplicables of the world; and at the things which she failed to understand, a category which included much natural science but less of human nature'.[15] As is well known, Russell continually wavered between atheism and agnosticism. Regardless, his admiration of Ottoline, coupled with his conviction that she possessed a special sort of insight into something truly good, led him to believe there must be something of value in her faith. The problem was that her admirable religious attitudes were attached to beliefs 'which there was no reason whatsoever for thinking true. To do so was to indulge in wishful thinking, or muddle-headedness or even intellectual dishonesty.'[16]

How could Russell preserve Ottoline's religious attitudes while jettisoning the beliefs to which they were attached? In 1911, he discussed the possibility of developing a non-credal religion – a means of settling their religious differences by developing a philosophy of religion that did not require commitment to fallacious religious beliefs. The work in which he planned to develop this quasi-mystical approach to understanding religious matters, *Prisons*, focused on religious *attitudes*, avoiding the matter of beliefs almost entirely. And it was a failure. It failed, as Griffin writes, because although Russell's talents lay in the justification and analysis of beliefs, 'If Russell was to avoid the sin of intellectual dishonesty himself, 'Prisons' had to confine itself strictly to attitudes. Attitudes could be recommended or not, but they could not, Russell thought, be argued for.'[17]

Although his non-credal religion was a failure, his emotivism seems to be a similar attempt at a non-credal moral philosophy that would reconcile ethics to his robust realism. Russell had already concluded that religious language could only be defensible if it expressed attitudes rather than beliefs, Griffin explains: 'In his effort to find some common ground with Ottoline . . . he had come to consider whether his theory of values could not be seen as just a different way of expressing Ottoline's religion.'[18] A letter written to Ottoline on 3 January 1912, indicates that he had begun to think about ethics non-cognitively – more than a year prior to the publication of Santayana's *Winds of Doctrine*. He writes:

Man can imagine things that don't exist, and sometimes he can see that they are better than things that do exist: this is involved in all rational action, which is the attempt to create imagined goods. What is disputable is the status of things merely imagined, still more of things merely possible to imagine but not actually imagined.[19]

Unless he is assuming something akin to emotivism, Russell's statements about nonexistent things are inconsistent with his own theory of descriptions. That theory, Griffin writes, 'held that all *statements* about what did not exist were false, [now] he says that the evaluation of some things that did not exist as better than some things that did was the basis of all rational action'.[20] This presents a problem, for if Russell is to be consistent, 'he must deny that these evaluations involve statements about what does not exist'.[21] The theory of descriptions, briefly, states that descriptions which denote imagined goods – such as the ideal person or the perfect legal system – denote nothing. Ethics involves, much of the time and perhaps necessarily, such phrases. Any subject-predicate sentence in which such phrases are the grammatical subject (such as, 'The perfect legal system is good'), analyzed by means of Russell's theory of descriptions, must be false. Even if there were such a property as goodness, there is nothing to bear it.[22] It would appear, then, that if ethical sentences are *statements* then they must be false. That, or they are not statements at all, but something else entirely.[23] By 1912, Russell must have realized that ethical statements presented a significant problem. His theory of descriptions did not sit well with Moore's intuitionist metaethic. Still, Russell's letter does not prove that he had actually adopted emotivism at this point, only that he had begun to lean in that direction.

The change of focus may have had something to do with a belief that a property of goodness is unnecessary as well. A few years later, in 1916, Russell stated that he was initially led to believe in ethical subjectivity 'by a number of reasons, some logical, some derived from observation. Occam's Razor . . . leads me to discard the notion of an absolute good if ethics can be accounted for without it.'[24] His observations of ethical judgments led him to believe that 'the claim of universality which men associate with their ethical judgments embodies merely the impulse to persecution or tyranny'.[25] The disgust evident in this last line grew out of the human cruelty Russell had witnessed in the years since 1912 – and a growing conviction that belief in absolute value *leads* people to become hateful and intolerant.

The seminal event in Russell's life was the advent of the First World War. The war was, in the end, the breaking point for his belief in ethical objectivity, leading him into activism and shaking his moral and philosophical convictions so deeply that he never recovered his intuitionist faith. Indeed, in an article written during the war, Russell explicitly states that personal reflection caused by the war led him to treat his own ethical opinions as mere emotive expressions.[26] He had always had an interest in political matters and practical ethics – politics was, after all, the family tradition; Russell had been raised in the expectation that he would follow in his grandfather's footsteps as Prime Minister. As Griffin writes:

> He had been active in the free trade controversy in 1904 and again in the campaign for women's suffrage in 1906–10. He had regularly campaigned in British elections, usually in support of the Liberals, and had once stood for election himself as a women's suffrage candidate. His first book had been a study of the German Social Democrats, and he had been keenly interested in the Boer War, during which he converted from an imperialist to a pro-Boer.[27]

But before the First World War, his political activity had been scattershot, and it had always taken a backseat to mathematical philosophy and an ivory-tower lifestyle. What shook him out of the tower – what had a profound personal, intellectual and political impact – was the sight of thousands of healthy young men marching off to slaughter and be slaughtered.

Kirk Willis explains the impact of the war rather eloquently in his introduction to the latest edition of Russell's *Power*. Russell viewed the First World War as 'an abomination; indeed, it offended his every moral precept and political instinct':

> He therefore threw himself into the neutrality campaign and then into the anti-war movement – speaking, writing, organizing, and counselling. And as the war lengthened and Britain's commitment extended, Russell's opposition sharpened – to the mistreatment of conscientious objectors, to the suppression of civil liberties, to the deceptions of the government, to the distortions of the press lords, and to the wastefulness of British commanders. This opposition – strident, unrelenting, and bitterly unpopular – was the defining experience of Russell's life. Not merely did emotions run so high on all sides that Russell alienated friends, exasperated allies, and enraged authorities, but he found himself – for the first time in his hitherto privileged life – the victim rather than the ally of the forces of authority. To his dismay and their discredit, for instance, the governing body of Trinity College – unable to bear his opinions any longer – dismissed him from his lectureship in 1916. And in the spring of 1918 he found himself imprisoned for six months because of an ill-tempered and jeering article he had written defaming Britain's new American ally.[28]

If Santayana's attacks and his own attempt to create a non-credal religion had led Russell to doubt objective morality and to search for a replacement, the First World War finally converted him. The last remnants of his intuitionist faith crumbled in the face of cruelty, suffering and fanaticism on a scale few could have imagined. In the face of mounting hatred and destruction, propped up by wilfully embraced propaganda, Russell, slipping into a devastating crisis of conscience, began to understand that the good was not as obvious as Moore's intuitionism made it out to be. Those around him, in England and all over the world, appealed to similar values, similar rules, and made similar accusations against one another. Each thought good was embodied in their own actions and causes, evil in the other's. The British regarded the Germans as wicked, and thought it good to slaughter them. Germans felt likewise about the British. Clearly, neither side was as wicked as the other claimed; both could not have understood the good correctly, if either had. Both sides neglected to seriously consider the other's point of view which, as one might expect, made simplistic assessments and commitment to slaughter all the easier.

Russell could not accept that either side was justified in its commitment to wholesale destruction. But he urged under-standing on deaf ears, as in these passages from letters to the editor of *The Cambridge Magazine,* written about one year apart:

> I cannot think that it is undesirable to try to understand the reasons which make the German and Austrian people believe – quite mistakenly, as we are convinced – that they have a good case in this war. No nation is wholly devilish or wholly angelic; where there is a national unanimity, there must be some general belief which seems to afford justification. I do not think we shall discover how to avert future wars so long as belligerent nations regard each other as simply wicked, and I cannot think that a good case suffers from justice and fair-mindedness.[29]

> The spirit of the German Government is hateful to me, but I see much of the same spirit in many Englishmen, and in them I mind it more, because the honour of England is more important to me than that of Germany. And although many

acts of the German Government and of individual German soldiers are hateful, I cannot believe that there is wisdom, or hope for the welfare of Europe, in hatred of the German nation. I think it is wholesome to realise that our Government, likewise, has done many hateful things, that all men have need of charity, and that a merely punitive justice is apt to make the judge as cruel as the criminal.[30]

Human nature turned out to be much darker than he had previously supposed. In a letter written to Ottoline during the war, he relates the conversation of two English soldiers he had observed on the train: 'One of them described, amid roars of laughter, how a German had knelt before him & besought mercy with tears, but he (the speaker) had put his bayonet through him. Perhaps he was boasting.'[31] That human beings could act with such indifference to the suffering of others, even take pleasure in it, shocked Russell's innocent liberal mind.

In order to understand 'the fierce and irrational hatred'[32] of his friends and neighbours toward Germany, and their enthusiasm in sending their sons and brothers to their deaths, Russell was forced to dispense with many more of his assumptions – among them, the Moorean assumption that human beings possess a natural intuitive apprehension of the Good. 'I had supposed until that time that it was quite common for parents to love their children,' he wrote, with a touch of irony, 'but the War persuaded me that it is a rare exception. I had supposed that most people liked money better than almost anything else, but I discovered that they liked death and destruction even better.'[33] The elite were just as disappointing: 'I had supposed that intellectuals frequently loved truth, but I found here again that not ten per cent of them prefer truth to popularity.'[34] The public, the politicians, the academics, everyone had betrayed their interests and their principles, and so 'I became filled with despairing tenderness towards the young men who were to be slaughtered, and with rage against all the statesmen of Europe'.[35]

The Music Swells

The period in which Russell turned to emotivism is one of tremendous turmoil, change and re-evaluation. At this stage we have the genesis of the universal sympathy and compassion that fuelled Russell's work in the decades to come. The renewed energy and focus he received from his relationship with Ottoline set him down this road, but also threw his mind into a confused state, setting the stage for his conversion to emotivism. Add to that the fact that he had always had doubts regarding intuitionism, strengthened by his disastrous attempts to apply it, by the gradual realization that a property of goodness may be unnecessary, and by the apparent incompatibility of intuitionism with his influential theory of descriptions, and the way has been prepared for Santayana's attack.

Finally, his attempt to create a non-credal religion in order to find common ground with Ottoline indicated a similar path in ethics, one that he might have thought seemed more promising than the disaster that was *Prisons*. He took that path, eventually bringing with him a preoccupation with desire and impulse that had always lurked in the back of his mind. Within a couple of decades, his synthesis of emotivism with his theories of desire and impulse would result in the most sophisticated and fascinating form of emotivism yet to appear.

First, however, he had to get his feet wet.

Notes

1. Thomas C. Kennedy, 'Nourishing life: Russell and the twentieth-century British peace movement, 1900–18', *Intellect and Social Conscience*, ed. Margaret Moran and Carl Spadoni (Hamilton: McMaster University Library Press, 1984), 224.

2. Charles Pigden, *Russell on Ethics* (London: Routledge, 1999), 9; henceforth 'Pigden, *RoE*'. Pigden makes the point that Russell, contrary to popular opinion, was involved in the creation and evolution of Moore's theory, though he was never an *orthodox* Moorean (see Russell's essay 'The elements of ethics'). The rest of Russell's intuitionist output can be found in 'Was the world good before the sixth day?' (Pigden, *RoE*, paper 12) and, of course, 'A free man's worship'. On a positive note, Russell does not appear to share any blame for the open-question argument.

3. See *ibid.*, paper 10: 'Is ethics a branch of empirical psychology?' Moore mercilessly attacked Russell's early attempts to define 'good' in terms of desire.

4. Bertrand Russell, *The Autobiography of Bertrand Russell: Volume Two, 1914–1944* (London: McClelland and Stewart Limited, 1968), 15; henceforth 'Russell, *Auto Two*'.

5. Pigden, *RoE*, 105.

6. George Santayana, *Winds of Doctrine*, 2nd edition (New York: Charles Scribner's Sons, 1926). In the second edition, Santayana's attack on Russell's moral philosophy can be found on pages 114–6 and 138–54. Although Santayana shies away from argument *per se*, extracting and constructing arguments out of his mockery is an easy task – they're *there*, lurking beneath his mask of cynical superficiality. And the book is thoroughly entertaining, at times hilarious.

7. Harry Ruja, 'Russell on the meaning of "good" ', in Moran and Spadoni, *Intellect and Social Conscience*, 137.

8. Ruja's article offers an excellent summary of Santayana's attack, and of Russell's pre-Moorean 'desire to desire' theory. However, he appears to misunderstand Russell's moral philosophy much of the time; especially his emotivism, which, Ruja claims, 'Russell did not advocate . . . prominently or continually' (ibid., 156) – though thirty years and a score of books and articles suggest otherwise.

9. Ibid., 140–1.

10. Ibid., 142.

11. There is nothing in Moore's ethics that would *necessarily* lead to such

a life, though it did for Russell. Then again, it is difficult to imagine an emotionally healthy Moorean.

12. Charles Pigden, 'Bertrand Russell: Moral philosopher or unphilosophical moralist?', *The Cambridge Companion to Bertrand Russell*, ed. Nicholas Griffin (Cambridge: Cambridge University Press, 2003), 499; henceforth 'Pigden, BR'.

13. Ronald Clark, *The Life of Bertrand Russell* (London: Jonathan Cape, Ltd., 1975), 132.

14. Ibid., 147.

15. Ibid., 157.

16. Nicholas Griffin, *The Selected Letters of Bertrand Russell: The Private Years, 1884–1914* (London: Routledge, 2002), 392.

17. Ibid., 392.

18. Ibid., 398.

19. Letter to Ottoline Morrell, 3 January 1912, # 184 in ibid., 400.

20. Ibid., 399. In this passage, 'all *statements*' should be corrected to read: 'all statements in which a description which lacked a denotation had a *primary* occurrence'.

21. Ibid., 399.

22. The most compatible metaethic, then, appears to be error theory – in which ethical sentences can have a truth-value, but they are always false. Russell pioneered error theory in 1922, though whether he actually embraced it is unclear.

23. The best, certainly the most famous, statement of the theory of descriptions (or a prototype of it) can be found in Russell's 'On denoting', a short and somewhat challenging paper published in 1905 and now found in many different anthologies. I have used Bertrand Russell, *Logic and Knowledge. Essays, 1901–1950*, ed. Robert C. Marsh (London: George Allen & Unwin, Ltd., 1956), 39–56. Although I have tried to give a brief, but accurate, statement of Russell's theory here, I'm sure anyone better versed in logic than I will find much to quarrel with. Those courageous souls looking for a mature version of the theory can find it in *Principia Mathematica*.

24. Bertrand Russell, 'North Staffs' praise of war', *Yours Faithfully, Bertrand Russell*, ed. Ray Perkins, Jr. (Chicago: Open Court, 2002), 59.

25. Ibid.

26. Bertrand Russell, 'War and non-resistance', in Pigden, *RoE*, 113.

27. Nicholas Griffin, *The Selected Letters of Bertrand Russell: The Public Years, 1914–1970* (London: Routledge, 2001), xvii.

28. Kirk Willis, 'Introduction', to Bertrand Russell, *Power* (London: Routledge, 1995), viii.
29. Russell in Perkins, *Yours Faithfully*, 38.
30. Russell in ibid., 54.
31. Ray Monk, *Bertrand Russell: The Spirit of Solitude* (London: Vintage/ Random House, 1997), 417.
32. Ibid., 367.
33. Russell, *Auto Two*, 17.
34. Ibid.
35. Ibid.

2

A Critique of Basic Emotivism

The First Foray

Although Pigden, among others, characterizes Russell's first foray out of intuitionism as a form of emotivism (Pigden calls it 'proto-emotivism'), it may be more accurate to describe Russell at this time as a simple subjectivist with emotivist tendencies, or as one who wavered between emotivism and simple subjectivism. In the present chapter we will examine the arguments of the most popular emotivists, A.J. Ayer and C.L. Stevenson, as well as some of the criticisms they face, and undertake a comparison of their theories to Russell's between 1913–22. Although Ayer and Stevenson were not the first to set out a form of emotivism – Barnes, Ogden and Richards are generally regarded as pioneers, and even they have predecessors in philosophy and psychology – nevertheless, they were emotivism's most influential proponents. By considering their theories in some detail, we will come to a greater appreciation of the superiority of Russell's emotivism, progressing as it did from the crude emotivism/subjectivism hybrid considered in this chapter to the deliciously refined emotivism we will examine in later chapters.

This chapter's subject matter is a parade of failure, though an interesting one. We will find that, although Ayer and Stevenson may be able to meet many of the common objections tossed their way, their theories are nonetheless inadequate. Russell's proto-emotivism, though it sometimes succeeds where Ayer's and Stevenson's fail, is inadequate and unconvincing for different reasons.

In particular, Russell's early theory fails because it is not much of a theory at all.

Foundations

Ayer's general position depends on his *verification principle*. According to this principle, a statement is only meaningful if it is either an analytic proposition, in which case it is necessarily true or necessarily false, or an empirical hypothesis, in which case at best it can only approximate truth. Regarding the latter category, Mary Warnock explains: 'Both the meaning and the probability of the hypothesis are established by empirical verification. That is to say, if a statement is to qualify for the second category, it must be capable of verification by sense-experience.'[1] Any statement that is neither true or false by definition nor verifiable by sense-experience is meaningless. Since ethical statements meet neither criterion, they can have no literal meaning. Ayer himself writes, 'in so far as statements of value are significant, they are ordinary "scientific" statements; and . . . in so far as they are not scientific, they are . . . simply expressions of emotion which can be neither true nor false'.[2] A significant statement, as Ayer understands it, is a statement with literal, cognitive, meaning – in other words, a statement capable of truth and falsity.

Philosophers, Ayer contends, routinely muddle their systems of ethics with bits of metaphysics, analyses of non-ethical concepts and terms,[3] and a potpourri of disparate ethical content (to use 'content' loosely). They would do well, he maintains, to distinguish among different classes of sentences commonly used in ethical writing and speaking:[4] one containing propositions defining ethical terms and judgments regarding the adequacy of proposed definitions; one containing propositions defining and explaining the phenomena of moral experience; one including 'exhortations to moral virtue' – the stock in trade of the moralist; and, finally, a fourth class containing ethical value judgments.

Ayer's startlingly narrow conception of philosophy – quite similar, in fact, to Russell's – appears to have backed ethical statements into a corner. Of the classes he has proposed, only the first 'can be said to constitute ethical philosophy', this is 'easy to see'.[5] For Ayer, philosophy's primary tasks are definition and its subsidiary, classification. The second class belongs to psychology and sociology. The third is the activity of preachers and propagandists, the issuing of commands designed to provoke listeners and readers to action. Such sentences belong to neither philosophy nor science. But the fourth class is not as easy to characterize – or degrade, as the case may be. Ayer does not know exactly where these judgments belong, only that since they are neither definitions, nor comments on definitions, nor quotations, they cannot be part of moral philosophy.

If Ayer has classified these different kinds of sentences correctly, he believes it follows that: 'A strictly philosophical treatise on ethics should therefore make no ethical pronouncement. But it should, by giving an analysis of ethical terms, show what is in the category to which all such pronouncements belong.'[6] And this is precisely what Ayer plans to do. He does not notice that he has not described the fourth set of sentences at all, merely told us how they should *not* be described. Given that this last set of sentences is the most important to the task at hand, once certainly wishes Ayer had not been so careless.[7]

Stevenson follows a different strategy. In 'The Emotive Meaning of Ethical Terms',[8] published in 1937, he proposes that such ethical questions as 'Is X good?' – which he understands as the *primary* form of ethical questions – are difficult to answer because they are unclear. We do not know what 'good' means, and so do not know what we are looking for, nor how we could even begin to search for an answer. He wishes to clarify ethical questions, and so writes: 'In order to help answer the question 'Is X good?' we must *substitute* for it a question which is free from ambiguity and confusion.'[9] We must try to find a question equivalent in all relevant respects to 'Is X good?' that is also unequivocally lucid.

Since the original question is unclear, we cannot expect its substitute to be strictly identical with it. Rather, 'The questions will be identical only in the sense that a child is identical with the man he later becomes.'[10] In mystical terms, one might say that the two questions are to be identical in spirit, or in essence, however they may differ in minor details. The original question and its substitute are to be related, roughly, by the replacement of 'good' by its definition. So we must ask: 'How must the defined meaning of "good" be related to its original meaning?'[11]

The defined meaning, Stevenson claims, must be *relevant* to the original meaning; that is, once one has understood the definition correctly, one must be able to use the term as defined without ever needing to revert to its former, vague, sense. If the original meaning was so confused that it could be used in several different senses, we must define several meanings for it – in which case only the complete set of definitions can be called 'relevant' (we could say, '*wholly* relevant'), each individual definition being 'partially relevant'.[12]

Stevenson's Three Requirements

Stevenson claims that any adequate definition of 'good' must comply with three common-sense requirements:

First, 'we must be able sensibly to *disagree* about whether something is "good"'.[13] Hobbes' simple subjectivist definition of the good as 'that which I desire' must go, for it makes disagreement – or, at least, contradiction – impossible. Similarly, the definition of 'good' as 'desired by my community or society' (which Stevenson identifies with Hume) is also excluded. Issues of disagreement and contradiction returned to haunt emotivists as the bases of several common objections.

Second, "goodness" must have, so to speak, a magnetism. A person who recognizes X to be "good" must *ipso facto* acquire a stronger tendency to act in its favour than he otherwise would have had.'[14] Once one knows that something is good, one must feel inclined to promote it, to act in accordance with it, and so forth. Consequently, Hume's definition – to call something "good" is to recognize that it enjoys the approval of the majority – must be rejected. One can recognize that the majority approve of a practice, yet reject it nonetheless.

Third, 'the "goodness" of anything must not be verifiable solely by use of the scientific method'.[15] Obviously, Ayer and Stevenson (Russell as well) walk hand-in-hand down this particular path. *Without* this requirement, Stevenson claims, ethics is little or nothing more than mere psychology, sociology, perhaps even biology. *With* this requirement, all interest theories (such as those of Hobbes and Hume) and naturalistic theories are banished. Stevenson admits: 'It is so sweeping a restriction that we must examine its plausibility. What are the methodological implications of interest theories which are here rejected?'[16]

Both Hume's and Hobbes' theories allow ethical judgments to be proven by appeal to empirical observation, and this is true even of the more complicated interest theories. If, for example, 'X is good' meant '*most people would approve of X if they knew its nature and consequences*', we would prove that X was good by first investigating X's nature and probable consequences, then determining whether most people would approve of what we had established of X's nature and probable consequences. All of this can be done empirically. Even so, it appears that 'the definition we have been considering has presupposed democratic ideals from the start; it has dressed up democratic propaganda in the guise of a definition'.[17] An aristocrat or radical individualist could simply refuse to consider the approval of the majority as relevant to goodness. Besides, I might add, the definition obviously presupposes that the democratic ideals it depends upon are 'good'. We may still inquire whether they are indeed 'good', in addition to asking why majority approval should matter at all. The answer may be that most people would say that majority approval is good, which is circular.

And that leads us to Stevenson's next point, that Moore's open-question argument devastates interest theory and establishes the importance of his third requirement. In Stevenson's words, Moore claims that: 'No matter what set of scientifically knowable properties a thing may have . . . you will find, on careful introspection, that it is an open question to ask whether anything having these properties is *good*.'[18] The fact that we can keep asking this question appears to indicate that 'we must be using some sense of "good" which is not definable, relevantly, in terms of anything scientifically knowable'.[19]

The Meanings and Uses of Ethical Terms

Stevenson believes his three common-sense requirements devastate interest theory, but what does he offer in its stead? He explains that he believes firmly in his requirements, and that they can be met by a kind of interest theory which gives up a presupposition made by all the others: namely, the presupposition 'that ethical statements are *descriptive* of the existing state of [attitudes] – that they simply *give information* about [attitudes]'.[20] Ayer is led to a similar conclusion. He believes that 'in our language, sentences which contain *normative* ethical symbols are not equivalent to sentences which express psychological propositions, or indeed empirical propositions of any kind'.[21] Note that

Ayer's claim applies only to normative ethical symbols; *descriptive* ethical symbols may be definable in factual terms. Confusion arises because the same language is used for both, yet the way in which a term is used indicates a difference between the two types of symbols. The statement 'X is wrong', Ayer writes, 'may constitute a sentence which expresses a moral judgment concerning a certain type of conduct, or it may constitute a sentence which states that a certain type of conduct is repugnant to the moral sense of a particular society'.[22] In the former case, 'wrong' is used as a normative ethical symbol, and the sentence is not an empirical proposition. But in the latter case, 'wrong' is used as a descriptive ethical symbol, and the sentence is a sociological or anthropological proposition, a statement of fact that can be true or false. In this case, one could say 'X is good', yet feel disapproval towards it, meaning only something along the lines of 'X is what passes for good in my society'. Russell, too, made frequent use of a distinction between what is good and what passes for good (usually as part of a sarcastic remark), so we ought to keep this distinction in mind as we progress.

Ayer and Stevenson agree, then, that moral judgments are something more than descriptions of one's attitude or emotions. Descriptive ethical symbols – and thus, descriptive ethical judgments – exist. We make such judgments. But we do not use moral judgments primarily to *describe*. The use of language has two purposes, Stevenson proposes: descriptive use, which is intended to communicate or record beliefs, and dynamic use, which is intended to express feelings, create moods or influence others.[23] Since the distinction between the two rests on the purpose of the particular language user, the same sentence may be used descriptively one day, dynamically the next. The same sentence may even have *different* dynamic uses at different times. Knowing whether a sentence is being used dynamically can be difficult, so one must pay attention not only to the words the language user employs, but also to 'his tone of voice, his gestures, the general circumstances under which he is speaking, and so on'.[24]

Often, Ayer admits, ethical words are used not to *express* an attitude but to *arouse* feelings or attitudes in others, to stir them to action or bend them to one's will – as, for example, when used by the propagandist, the preacher and the courtroom lawyer. They can be used in this way to turn a sentence into a command. 'It is your duty to tell the truth', writes Ayer, both expresses a feeling and includes the command, 'Tell the truth'. 'You ought to . . .' and 'It is good to . . .' can be similarly used, though each is less emphatic than its predecessor. We may 'define the meaning of the various ethical words in terms both of the different feelings they are ordinarily taken to express, and also the different responses which they are calculated to provoke'.[25]

Whereas Ayer recognizes that ethical judgments can be used to influence people, he does so almost as an aside. Stevenson, on the other hand, believes that influencing the attitudes of others is the *primary function* of ethical judgments. Yes, ethical statements may contain an element of description, but: 'Their major use is not to indicate facts, but to *create an influence.* Instead of merely describing people's [attitudes], they *change* or *intensify* them. They *recommend* an [attitude in] an object, rather than state that the [attitude] already exists.'[26] When I tell my son he should never kill anyone, that killing is bad, my intention is not to inform him that I disapprove of killing. I intend to lead *him* to disapprove of killing as well. I wish to influence him, modify his interests or create new ones, perhaps. If he does not come to share my disapproval of killing, I will not tell myself that I've convinced him that killing is wrong, even though he acknowledges that I, and perhaps society, disapprove of killing. No, I will tell myself that I *failed* to convince him that killing is wrong. If I attempt to convince him by an appeal to the consequences of killing, I use these reasons as 'a means of facilitating' my influence. And if I thought that an appeal to consequences would not affect his attitude at all, I would not make it. Stevenson adds: 'So the consideration about other people's [attitudes] is just an additional means you may employ, in order to move him, and is not part of the ethical judgment itself.'[27]

We find that people come to use ethical statements differently due to their social influences – external influences as great as the countries and historical circumstances in which they were raised, as quaint as their families and churches. To a great extent, such influences operate upon us through words: 'People praise one another, to encourage certain inclinations, and blame one another, to discourage others. Those of forceful personalities issue commands which weaker people, for complicated instinctive reasons, find it difficult to disobey, quite apart from fears of consequences'[28] – not to mention the influence of rhetoric used by writers and orators. Ethical terms are particularly effective in suggestion, and the reason, Stevenson believes, that two people from the same community have more in common when it comes to moral attitudes than two people from different communities is that 'ethical judgments propagate themselves. One man says "This is good"; this may influence the approval of another person, who then makes the same ethical judgment, which in turn influences another person, and so on.'[29] And, of course, this process *lends a veneer of objectivity* to the moral judgments passed around as common-sense wisdom. Although Stevenson's idea contains some truth, I expect the full explanation is not so simple.

Ayer believes that 'the fundamental ethical concepts are unanalysable, inasmuch as there is no criterion by which one can test the judgments in which they occur', and he believes he has dealt with the matter in his refutations of simple subjectivism and utilitarianism.[30] But why is there no criterion? Because – and at this point he and Stevenson part ways – ethical terms 'are mere pseudo-concepts'[31] that add nothing to the factual content of any proposition in which they occur. As Warnock restates it:

'The predicates used in value judgments are not proper predicates; they do not stand for qualities of things which can be picked out by the senses.'[32] Take the sentence, 'You were *wrong* to kill Billy'. What fact does that sentence tell us that 'You killed Billy' does not? It tells us nothing about the act itself. All it adds is an expression of disapproval, of an emotion or attitude, nothing more. Now transform that sentence into a general ethical statement: 'Killing is wrong'. It has no factual meaning. It cannot be true or false. One may as well write 'Killing!', hoping to express shock or horror or disapproval with the subtle power of an exclamation point. 'Killing!' says just as much as 'Killing is wrong' – that is, according to the verification principle, it says nothing strictly meaningful. It is not a judgment at all, merely an expression of attitude.

Ayer is not a simple subjectivist, of course; he wishes to make it clear that moral judgments are not *assertions that* one has a feeling. 'Killing is wrong' does not mean 'I disapprove of killing'. He acknowledges that the task of distinguishing between the *expression of* a feeling and the *assertion that* one has a feeling can be difficult, for they often skip hand-in-hand; after all, I can express pain and assert that I feel pain in the same utterance. However, I can also express pain without making an assertion – with grimaces, gestures, inarticulate cries while I talk about the weather. One may also assert that one has a feeling without expressing it, but Ayer believes this is rare.[33]

Sir David Ross attacks Ayer's contention that ethical judgments are merely expressions of attitude. 'If that were all they were,' Ross asks, 'why argue at all? What should we be trying to prove? Is A arguing to prove that he likes the given act, and B to prove that he dislikes it?'[34] That doesn't make sense to Ross, for one is not likely to doubt that the other is arguing the contrary position simply out of spite. Their intent is to convince one another that the object of their dispute *deserves* to be liked or disliked. Yet, Ayer might ask, why should their intent matter? If this is what they believe and intend, they are obviously mistaken as to the nature of moral judgments. Their intention betrays a false belief in ethical objectivity that has nothing to do with the actual meaning of their moral statements. They are like tourists mimicking phrases heard in a foreign land. Though they may use the phrases correctly, in their proper context, they are oblivious to their precise meaning. That people use words in a certain way, believing they have certain meanings, does not prove that they actually *have* those meanings. To say people believe otherwise is no objection – any more than it would be if I reacted to the assertion that schizophrenics do not *really* hear the voice of God by insisting, 'But they *believe* they do!'

One might respond by insisting that, were I to ask someone to explain what a horse is and he responded, 'Well, the most striking things about them are their soft feathers and the way they fly from tree to tree, building nests and laying eggs', we would assume he was talking about birds, not horses. We would not take him seriously were he to object to our judgment of him by protesting, 'No, that's how horses really are! I know that everyone thinks they are large hairy quadrupeds that sometimes jump but never fly, but I assure you they are quite wrong. Horses really are a species of bird.' Such examples, amusing though they are, miss two crucial points. First, the vast majority of us have observed a horse (at least in pictures), and can point to commonly observed properties among all examples of the species that bind them together in a common class yet distinguish them from other classes of animals, vegetables and minerals. Second, there is no serious controversy regarding what is to count as a horse, largely because of the previous point. That is, there is an overwhelming general consensus as to what may be called a horse.

In ethics, there is no equivalent general consensus upon which we can rely. It is now quite common to hear an undergraduate blithely declare that moral judgments have no meaning, or mean only that I (or my society, or my religion, etc.) feel a certain way about something. The meanings of ethical terms and the status of ethical judgments are controversial – in large part *because* there are no physical characteristics to which we can point. This is true even though most of us are inclined to disapprove of the same things. The fact that most people are inclined to call baby-tossing 'bad' may be irrelevant to the question of what 'bad' *means*.

Furthermore, in response to the question of why anyone would bother engaging in an ethical dispute if there were no truths at stake, Ayer and Stevenson both state that ethical terms and judgments may be used to *persuade* others to change their attitudes to match one's own. There is, then, a point to ethical disputes.

Perhaps Ross could respond by insisting that words must mean what they are generally understood to mean, that we cannot give them a meaning other than that which is commonly understood. To that I would reply (though Ayer may not agree) that we cannot possibly know, with any accuracy, what some words are 'commonly understood' to mean. Leaving aside words that may not have an independent meaning at all, e.g. definite articles, contentious words such as 'good' and 'right' admit of several possible meanings – hence employment opportunities for philosophers. Whom do we poll to discover the 'common meaning'?[35] When we receive the results, which of the multiple 'meanings' discovered do we accept as the 'common' one? Not only is the contention that words mean what they are commonly understood to mean *false*, and not only do we have no reason to believe it, but we can't even begin to put it into practice. Its status is that of an ethical exhortation upon which it is impossible to act.

Take, for instance, the word 'borrow'. Some people use the word in the following way, 'I borrowed him twenty dollars so he could borrow it to his mother'. The meaning implied here (that 'to borrow' and 'to lend' are equivalent) is now common in some circles – just watch daytime television. In other circles, a more dictionary-friendly meaning reigns. So what does 'borrow' mean? Granted, the latter meaning is much more common than the first, so is that what 'borrow' is 'generally taken' to mean, and thus what it means *per se*?

If we answer yes, we commit the democratic fallacy – assuming that the latter meaning is the 'correct' one *because* most people use it in that way. It may actually be the correct meaning – I expect it is – but the fact that the meaning is the most common, the fact that more people 'generally understand' the word in the dictionary-friendly sense, does not, in itself, make it so. Furthermore, there is a 'people like us' factor at work. Which group's usage are we going to accept as 'correct'? We have a wide range of groups from which to choose, groups identified by nationality and class and education level, among others.

Finally, we must distinguish between what a word *means*, and how a word is *used*. I am inclined to believe that the strategy of identifying meaning with usage hit its natural dead end decades ago. Nonetheless, were Ross to offer a reason to take this strategy seriously, we would be forced to respond to his argument. Perhaps, in the end, he would convince us. Since he does not bother to make the effort, I will offer a possibility. In the case at hand, for instance, it may be that we commonly use ethical terms and judgments as though they were objective, capable of truth-values, and had some sort of compulsive power.[36] But that does not necessarily have anything to do with the *meaning* of an ethical term or judgment. Stevenson appears to agree with at least this point.

The dynamic uses of words and the meanings of those words, Stevenson claims, are not identical. The meaning of a word must be identified with the psychological causes and effects (such as inner experiences and dispositions) with which it *tends* to be connected – meaning 'is a causal or dispositional property of the word'.[37] And this tendency 'must exist for all who speak the language; it must be persistent and must be realizable more or less independently of determinate circumstances attending the word's utterance'.[38] When a word tends to express or arouse cognitive states of mind, we may say it has *descriptive* meaning. When a word tends to express or arouse affective states of mind, we may call its meaning *emotive*. A term may have both emotive and descriptive meaning, as do moral terms (and sentences, by extension), and the descriptive meaning may change without causing any change in the emotive meaning.

Emotive meaning has 'an intimate relation to dynamic usage'.[39] The emotive meaning of a term or phrase is 'a strong and persistent tendency, built up in the course of linguistic history, to give direct expression . . . to certain of the speaker's feelings or emotions or attitudes', and to evoke them in others.[40] Emotive meaning leads us to call some words laudatory, some derogatory – indicating whether an object or action is considered 'good' or 'bad', 'right' or 'wrong'. The word 'alas' tends to produce the same affective response in all who know English, and to use it to express merriment would be next to impossible; one would not be understood. The tendency of a word to produce certain affective responses is persistent and resilient, and so we may call it the word's 'meaning'.

Emotionally-laden words, such as 'lie', 'become suited, on account of their emotive meaning, to a certain kind of dynamic use. . . . The more pronounced a word's emotive meaning is, the less likely people are to use it purely descriptively.'[41] This does not mean that the dynamic use of a word is *identical* with its meaning – dynamic uses come and go with the speaker's intention; they are far less stable than emotive meanings. On the other hand, 'there is an important contingent relationship between emotive meaning and dynamic purpose: the former assists the latter'.[42] If we define words like 'good' or 'bad' without making explicit their emotive meanings, we mislead people into thinking that the primary use of the word is descriptive, rather than dynamic.

For the moment, Stevenson will take 'X is good' to mean '*we like* X'.[43] Now, this latter sentence must be understood as used descriptively and dynamically, both describing a fact about the speaker's attitude, giving expression to it, and seeking to change the attitudes of others. It is being used to put forth a subtle suggestion: 'we' includes both the speaker and listener. The speaker hopes that the listener will (come to) share his approval of X. However, 'Even when "we like it" is used for suggestion, it is not quite like "this is good".'[44] The former neglects emotive meaning, whereas ' "good" has a laudatory emotive meaning that fits it for the dynamic use of suggesting favourable [attitudes]' – a subtle, indirect suggestion.[45] The problem is that there are no direct synonyms for 'good'. At best, Stevenson believes, we can approximate it with such words as 'desirable' or 'likeable', which do not express the same attitude and distort emotive meaning.

Ethical sentences allow us to influence others subtly, indirectly, perhaps unconsciously. An ethical sentence 'centers the hearer's attention not on his [attitudes] but on the subject of [his attitude], and thereby facilitates suggestion. [And] an ethical sentence readily permits counter-suggestion and leads to the give and take situation that is so characteristic of arguments about values.'[46]

Stevenson maintains that the closest we can come to a definition of 'good', is 'that "this is good" is *about* the favourable interest of the speaker and the hearer or hearers, and that it has a laudatory emotive meaning which fits the words for use in suggestion'.[47] That is as close as it gets – it clarifies the term's meaning and use, and that will have to do. Furthermore, the moral use of 'good' suggests more than mere liking; one who morally approves of something 'experiences a rich feeling of security when it prospers and is indignant or "shocked" when it does not'.[48] What would it mean for something that I like to prosper? It could mean that others come to like it as well. I am often driven to share the things I like and approve of, to spread the word about them, to convince others to feel the way I do. If I am successful, I get a vicarious sense of satisfaction from their new attitude toward the object of my approval. I feel, rightly or wrongly, justified in my attitude when it is shared by others.

One could object that, although I may like whiskey, it doesn't make sense to say that I want to 'see whiskey prosper'. What would it mean for whiskey to prosper? Perhaps Seagram's announces record profits. Yet what I'm interested in is readily available whiskey, not the wealth of its makers.

But would only 'moral persons' feel such a wish for prosperity? Such a question has little, if any, meaning in Stevenson's theory (much less in Ayer's). If one approves of segregation, one is pleased to see it prosper, one feels a sense of security in its enforcement. Each of us has 'moral' sentiments on this analysis, so each of us is 'moral' – though one may find the moral sentiments of others personally repugnant. The strength of one's approval may come into play; perhaps moral approval could be distinguished from mere liking by the strength of satisfaction one feels when the object of approval prospers. Even so, we are all 'moral' in some sense.

Disputes and Disagreements

Does Stevenson's proposed 'definition' meet his three requirements?[49] That it satisfies the second requirement strikes him as so obvious that it barely warrants comment. Succinctly, the second requirement demands only that the attitude of the speaker be included in the definition of 'good'. Since the attitude of the speaker is *part* of the emotive meaning, Stevenson has nothing to worry about on this front.

The other two requirements relate to moral disputes, or disagreements. Both Ayer and Stevenson spend a great deal of time
on this subject. In the course of their explanations, each reveals
some of the more subtle aspects of his theory. It is on this matter,
additionally, that both face the most common attacks.

There is obvious disagreement over ethical matters, Stevenson
writes. But is it 'disagreement in belief' or 'disagreement in
attitude'?[50] The former is typical of the natural sciences, the
latter of ethics. In a disagreement in belief, for example, I
believe that squirrels are merciless killers and you do not (or you
believe that my belief is false). It is this sort of disagreement
critics of emotivism tend to have in mind when they argue that it
renders disagreement impossible, Stevenson claims, for they
presuppose that disagreement entails contradiction and logical
incompatibility. But, in another example, if I have a favourable
attitude toward squirrels and you have an unfavourable attitude
toward them, we have a disagreement in attitude; beliefs need
not be involved.

Thus, ethical disagreements proper are disagreements in
attitude, cases in which the attitudes of two or more people are
incompossible. If I say caring for orphans is good and you say it is
bad, 'we have a case of suggestion and counter-suggestion'.[51] We
are each trying to change the other's attitude toward orphans.
We disagree in the sense that our different attitudes lead to
conflicting goals: I want you to share my attitude, you want me to
share yours. We cannot both be satisfied.

Stevenson admits that sometimes two parties in an ethical
dispute can resolve their disagreement empirically, and sometimes they cannot. Still, 'even when they can, the relation
between empirical knowledge and ethical judgments is quite
different from the one that traditional interest theories seem to
imply'.[52] Ethical judgments are implicit commands; as Warnock
explains it: 'If I am commanding you to like something by telling
you that it is good, the question how I get to know that it is good

need not arise.'[53] Nonetheless, intelligent people argue in an ethical dispute by attempting to support their judgments with 'reasons'. These reasons make appeals to beliefs and desires that the disputants hold, and it is in this way that ethical disagreements are sometimes resolved empirically (echoing Ayer). In other words, 'disagreement in [attitude] may be rooted in disagreement in belief. . . . people who disagree in [attitude] would often cease to do so if they knew the precise nature and consequences of the object of their [attitude]'.[54] Thus, we may be able to resolve some disagreements in attitude by effecting agreement in belief. Each party may try to fully describe the relevant features of the object of their dispute in the hope that a 'better' understanding of that object will lead the other to share his attitude. Yet, although the empirical method is in this manner relevant to ethics, 'empirical facts are not inductive grounds from which the ethical judgment problematically follows'.[55]

The empirical method is insufficient for solving ethical disputes. It works insofar as a disagreement in attitude stems from disagreement in belief. But many ethical disagreements are rooted in something else – for example, in personal characteristics (such as sympathy versus indifference toward suffering), or in social class. Although there is no rational method to settle such disputes, we may try to resolve them by changing our adversary in some way – through rhetoric, emotional appeals, eloquent and moving description or other forms of manipulation (or 'persuasion', if one prefers). Stevenson does not pour scorn on such tactics, since they are essential to the primary purpose of ethical judgments, as he understands them. He writes that 'it is only through such means that our personalities are able to grow, through our contact with others'.[56]

Ayer, similarly, takes great care in emphasizing that the lack of ethical truth and falsity does not imply that two people cannot disagree on moral issues. We may have different sentiments when it comes to killing; thus we may disagree – but you cannot

contradict me. Each party is simply expressing his moral sentiments. 'So', Ayer expands, 'there is plainly no sense in asking
which of us is in the right, for neither of us is asserting a genuine
proposition.'[57] All normative ethical symbols – 'good', 'bad',
'right', 'wrong', etc. – have this emotive character. They express
a feeling about, or attitude toward, an object; but they assert
nothing, cannot be true or false, and have no objective validity,
at least not when used in sentences containing ethical
judgments.

Which leads us to the only objection to emotivism that Ayer
takes seriously, one raised by Moore against simple subjectivism.
Namely, 'that if ethical statements were simply statements about
the speaker's feelings, it would be impossible to argue about
questions of value'.[58] In other words, emotivism makes it
impossible to have moral disputes. Obviously, the objection goes,
since we have moral disputes quite frequently, ethical statements
must be more than mere expressions of one's feelings or attitudes – or something else entirely.

But, Ayer says, it is not obvious that we have moral disputes – at
least, disputes over value. He claims that we never actually dispute questions of value; we dispute questions of fact *related* to
questions of value. In such disputes we do not try to show the
other that he has the 'wrong' feeling towards an object, issue or
question that he has correctly understood. Instead, we try to
show him that he does not fully understand the matter, that he
has misinterpreted or misunderstood the facts, overlooked significant information, misjudged or misconceived someone's
motive, miscalculated the effects of an action ('or its probable
effects in view of the agent's knowledge'),[59] or failed to take into
account extenuating circumstances. Or we try to argue about the
effects an action is likely to produce, 'or the qualities which are
usually manifested in their performance'.[60] In short, we hope or
expect that our adversary, by coming to appreciate the facts as we
do, will come to share our attitudes.

Since 'the people with whom we argue have generally received the same moral education as ourselves, and live in the same social order, our expectation is usually justified'.[61] If our adversary persists in disagreeing with us, whatever the cause may be, we tend to abandon our efforts to convince him through argument. Instead:

> We say that it is impossible to argue with him because he has a distorted or undeveloped moral sense; which signifies merely that he employs a different set of values from our own. We feel that our own system of values is superior, and therefore speak in such derogatory terms of his. But we cannot bring forward any arguments to show that our system is superior. For our judgment that it is so is itself a judgment of value, and accordingly outside the scope of argument. It is because argument fails us when we come to deal with pure questions of value, as distinct from questions of fact, that we finally resort to mere abuse.[62]

Perhaps my personal experience differs from Ayer's, for I have not found that most people resort to abuse when dealing with questions of value. Many people do, of course. But they need not, nor is it the norm. I expect we all know several people who can deal with such issues in a calm, reasonable manner. Then again, the means with which disputes are handled are of trivial import, since one may be calm and irrational in the same moment. Ayer is claiming that the only alternative to rational argument is abuse, which clearly isn't so. Avoiding abuse makes an argument civil, not rational.

Ayer approaches the issue differently in the introduction to the second edition of *Language, Truth and Logic*. There he writes, 'the common objects of moral approval or disapproval are not particular actions so much as classes of actions', that is, when we call an action right or wrong, we assume it belongs to a certain

class, the members of which share common characteristics.[63]
The statements of fact he wrote of earlier are statements of
'factual classification', placing an action into a class of actions
that typically arouse a 'certain moral attitude' in the speaker –
persuasive classification, if you will.[64] And so, 'a man who is a
convinced utilitarian may simply mean by calling an action right
that . . . it is the sort of action that tends to promote the general
happiness', in which case we can empirically investigate the statement's validity.[65] The language used in such factual statements
is the same as that used in normative sentences – hence the
common belief that normative statements are factual. Further
confusion results from the fact that many normative sentences
also contain some factual element or other, perhaps a description of the action being praised or condemned.

However, even if it were true that people could not contradict
each other on questions of value, 'it does not follow from this
that two persons cannot significantly disagree about a question
of value, or that it is idle for them to attempt to convince one
another'.[66] Surely we may disagree without formally contradicting one another and, if our goal is to change our adversary's
attitude, it is not necessary to contradict any assertions he makes
– to do so might even be counterproductive. Other tactics are
available, tactics we make use of quite frequently. As Stevenson
explained, we may try to alter our adversary's perception of the
case by pointing out facts he has overlooked or misunderstood.
Or we can manipulate him with carefully chosen emotive language – like the preacher, propagandist and courtroom lawyer
already mentioned. Ayer calls this 'a practical justification for the
use of normative expressions of value', and he, like Russell and
Stevenson, declines to refer to it as manipulation.[67]

The point is that argument about moral issues is possible only
if all concerned assume a common system of values. Ayer
explains:

If our opponent concurs with us in expressing moral disapproval of all actions of a given type *t*, then we may get him to condemn a particular action A, by bringing forward arguments to show that A is of type *t*. For the question whether A does or does not belong to that type is a plain question of fact. Given that a man has certain moral principles, we argue that he must, in order to be consistent, react morally to certain things in a certain way.[68]

When it comes to those principles themselves, no argument is possible.[69] For example, if you and I both hold the principle that all killing is wrong, yet I approve of sport hunting, you might try to convince me that sport hunting is a type of killing. Once this has been pointed out, my veil of ignorance having been lifted, I concur with you. Yes, sport hunting is a form of killing, and killing is wrong. However, when it comes to our shared principle – 'Killing is wrong' – there can be no argument. We agree only in our attitude toward killing; there is no truth or falsity in the expression of that common attitude.

Ross and Pigden take issue with the contention that dispute comes to an end once we reach the principles or values behind our attitudes. Although *argument* – that is, the exchange of reasons in support of our attitudes – may cease at that point, Ross writes, 'we do not find that all difference of opinion has vanished, and that we are left only with different feelings, one liking certain consequences or motives and another disliking them'.[70] Instead, disputants continue to disagree, one calling x 'good', the other calling it 'bad'. Ayer must show that all dispute – or 'difference of opinion' – ceases at this point, not merely argument.[71] I expect Ayer could respond to Ross by claiming that the parties continue to believe they have a moral dispute when in fact they do not. They are misled by the common belief that ethical judgments are judgments of fact, and so erroneously believe they are *disputing* a question of fact even though there is no longer any actual dispute. In another sense, though, they do have a moral dispute – because they recommend incompatible attitudes. Perhaps we could call it a 'dispositional dispute' (because there is not enough alliteration in philosophy).

Pigden's statement of this objection (echoing Moore) is more effective, but still fruitless. He writes, 'if moral judgments merely express feelings of approval and disapproval, they cannot contradict one another. Since 'X is bad' and 'X is good,' when said by different people, plainly *do* contradict one another, emotivism must be false.'[72] The terms 'good' and 'bad' are plainly contradictory, and we cannot properly resort to stipulative definitions in order to weasel our way out of the matter. Pigden seems to be using definitions of 'good' and 'bad' quite different from Ayer's. Simply stating that it is 'plain' or 'obvious' that the two statements contradict one another gets us nowhere. He must explain how. In Ayer's view, attitudes cannot contradict each other; it makes no sense to suppose that they do. What would it mean to say that two attitudes can contradict each other?[73]

One might argue that the attitudes do *not* contradict each other. That is, the emotive meanings of 'X is good' and 'X is bad' are not contradictory. But if these sentences contain descriptive meaning, as both Ayer and Stevenson allow, then in that sense they *do* contradict. The dispute, then, may be one of classification. Once we take this route, we have abandoned Pigden's argument (which relies on the antecedent, 'if moral judgments merely express feelings of approval and disapproval . . .'). So, do we have a substantial objection? No, for both Stevenson and Ayer have a ready rebuttal: their point is that, once the dispute has moved beyond the level of classification and descriptive meanings – once it has reached the level of basic principles – it vanishes. No more dispute. At this level, there is no longer any descriptive meaning.

Although the objection does not seem to work, it suggests that something is missing in Ayer's and Stevenson's theories – and that something is the contradiction in *fact* that we, rightly or wrongly, assume to be present in such disagreements. The emotivism of Ayer and Stevenson cannot account for our belief in ethical facts, in ethical knowledge. Since these beliefs play a key role in how we normally understand moral disputes, a satisfactory theory must be able to explain them.

Wellman takes the existence of ethical disagreement as evidence of 'a *claim* to rationality built into ethical statements'.[74] Stevenson, he asserts (and by extension, Ayer), cannot explain ethical disagreement because he has robbed ethical statements of their claim to rationality. Instead, Stevenson proposes that ethical disagreement arises when two people have incompossible[75] attitudes toward the same object and one of them, at least, wishes to change the other's attitude. Wellman is suspicious of the latter condition, accusing Stevenson of using it to gloss over the fact that some people have ethical differences without disagreement.

According to Stevenson, when two people have incompossible attitudes but neither wishes to change the other's attitude, there is no disagreement, or dispute. Those with incompossible attitudes may tolerate each other's opposite attitude. Not so, claims Wellman, for 'it often happens that two people argue strenuously about some ethical issue only to find that neither can convince the other. At this point both may give up and "agree to disagree"'.[76] Now neither of the two plans on changing the other's attitude (apparently because they realize the effort is futile, though this does not seem to follow), but they still disagree – they disagree without dispute. If both parties gave up the desire to change the other's interests, their attitudes would be compossible. And what if I believe killing is wrong, and you believe it is right, yet neither of us can be bothered to try converting the other? Perhaps we are lazy or apathetic. As Wellman states it: 'Their disagreement lies in the opposition of their attitudes; whether either has any real motive to overcome this opposition is quite another thing.'[77]

But Stevenson cannot make use of that last insight, for he does not allow for 'any logical opposition between attitudes'.[78] Stevenson's emotivism allows attitudes to conflict in a practical sense – they are incompossible; both cannot be satisfied. Wellman believes he has overlooked the fact that opposed attitudes may sometimes both be capable of satisfaction. He uses the example of a husband and wife, one of whom – the husband – enjoys kippers at breakfast, while the other does not. No worries – he can eat kippers for breakfast and she can have something else. In such cases, Wellman writes, 'the opposition between the attitudes even furthers the practical cooperation; for if both liked kippers, they would have to fight over who is to get the larger portion'.[79] How can this be? It can be because Stevenson is incorrect – 'the opposition of attitudes does not consist in the impossibility of satisfying both, for there are fortunate cases in which opposed attitudes need not conflict in practice'.[80] Ethical attitudes, rather, are logically opposed. 'X is good' claims that the rational attitude to take toward X is one of favour or desire, while 'X is bad' claims the opposite. Logically, both cannot be correct, and that is the ethical disagreement. And this implies that reasoning has a privileged role in ethical disagreement, a role far more important and exalted than the pragmatic, manipulative methods Stevenson suggests using.

Wellman's argument relies on an inadequate analogy and a complete misunderstanding of how Stevenson characterizes moral claims. Ethical disagreements involve more than do disagreements over kippers. Whereas in a disagreement over kippers, both parties can be satisfied because their attitudes need not involve a practical conflict (unless perhaps the wife disapproves of the *husband's* love of kippers), moral disagreements necessarily involve a practical conflict. The attitudes of two parties to a moral dispute are *necessarily* incompossible. According to

Stevenson's analysis, if I say 'killing is wrong' and another says 'killing is right', we hold contrary attitudes to killing – connected perhaps to descriptive beliefs about the class of actions to which killing belongs, its causes and consequences, etc. – *and* we both wish to change the other's attitude; indeed, we both wish for everyone in the world to adopt our attitudes, which rules out the case of disagreement without dispute.[81] It is immediately apparent that there is no motive to change the other's attitude in the case Wellman describes, because, as he points out, so long as they differ, each can be satisfied. This is simply not the case in an ethical dispute. I am certainly not likely to be satisfied if my adversary continues to flit about singing the praises of killing. I desire her to change her attitude.[82] Explicitly or implicitly, moral claims are universalized.

Pecking Away

The strongest objection to Ayer's emotivism targets its dependence on the verification principle. If we accept the weak interpretation of the verification principle, we need only establish that some evidence or observations are relevant to determining the truth-value of a proposition. If so, the proposition may be classified as an *empirical* proposition, though its truth-value could never be established with certainty. It appears, then, that ethical judgments, in the *descriptive* sense, may be classified as analytic *or* empirical, since it is possible that some observation is relevant in determining whether an act should be classified as 'right' or 'wrong'. On the other hand, we may classify acts as 'right' or 'wrong' by considering their definitions – primarily an analytic task. Murder, for instance, is commonly held to be 'bad' or 'wrong' by definition, since it can be roughly defined as 'wrongful killing'. True and useless.

Ayer, however, has argued that the verification principle

renders normative ethical judgments strictly meaningless, incapable of truth or falsity. His theory stands or falls with the verification principle – which we may not need to bother with anyway, since it is generally rejected now. As many have pointed out since *Language, Truth, and Logic* was published, the principle itself is not analytic, since it is not a definition, but a purported statement of fact. Nor is it empirical, because no observational evidence is relevant to its truth or falsity. Thus, according to itself, the verification principle is meaningless. A satisfactory emotivism must be established without resort to the verification principle if it is to succeed.

Wellman set forth quite clearly one of the most common objections to emotivism, which he uses as the basis for a set of related objections – namely, that ethical language *appears* to be objective, and we typically use it *believing* that it is objective. If emotivists are correct about ethical statements, he asks, 'why are they not formulated in the exclamatory or imperative mood? If they are neither true nor false, why do we speak of them as such? If logic is inapplicable to them, what are ethical arguments?'[83] As Wellman understands it, the mere appearance and assumption of objectivity in ethics is *prima facie* reason to believe that ethical statements are objective, and 'the mere fact that the appearance needs explaining is *prima facie* evidence against emotivism'.[84] He takes Stevenson to task for attempting to explain away the appearance of ethical objectivity while denying that ethical statements have any real objectivity whatsoever. His plan is to point out every little weakness he can find in Stevenson's case in order to establish its insufficiency. There is nothing wrong with the death-by-pinpricks strategy – and Wellman is quite correct to doubt emotivism's ability to explain moral phenomena. Ultimately, however, his objection is unconvincing.

Stevenson's theory, Wellman claims, is incapable of analyzing epistemic terms in relation to ethics. We tend to speak of ethical statements as true or false, of ethical conclusions as correct or incorrect, we call ethical arguments valid or invalid, and we distinguish between relevant and irrelevant reasons for a given ethical conclusion. If ethical statements have no objectivity, and lack a truth-value, how can our use of such terms be explained? According to Stevenson's theory, only the descriptive meaning of an ethical sentence can be true or false; the emotive meaning lacks a truth-value. As a whole, then, we cannot speak of an ethical sentence as true or false. In *Facts and Values*, Stevenson argued, in Wellman's words, 'that one can infer nothing about the function, meaning, or objectivity of an utterance from the fact that it can be spoken of as true or false because the applicability of these terms is determined solely by grammatical structure'.[85] Wellman finds this doubtful; I find it quite good. We speak of ethical sentences as true or false because we *assume* they are declaratives – and, grammatically, that's how we speak of declaratives. Whether or not they actually are declaratives is another issue. And we can legitimately speak of ethical arguments as valid or invalid when it comes to the *descriptive* meaning of ethical terms and sentences. Wellman says nothing of any consequence against such points, only that he finds it 'evident that one cannot speak of every declarative utterance as true or false' and that the possibility of every declarative sentence having a truth-value conflicts with his 'linguistic sense'.[86] It does not bother my 'linguistic sense', nor, apparently, did it bother Stevenson's. Perhaps Wellman has in mind the fact that *meaningless* declarative sentences are neither true nor false. In that case, I would agree with him, for my 'linguistic sense' is not bothered by the possibility of every *meaningful* declarative sentence having a truth-value. But we are not discussing meaningless sentences here; neither Stevenson nor Wellman is claiming that ethical sentences are meaningless.[87]

But a related, and rather interesting, objection to Stevenson's emotivism, raised by Wellman and Pigden, is that formal logic cannot be applied to ethical arguments.[88] Stevenson claims that an ethical argument – such as: anything that promotes liberty is good; education promotes liberty; therefore, education is good – can be valid and analyzed according to his first pattern of analysis.[89] But, Wellman asks, how can this argument be valid if neither the major premise nor the conclusion has a truth-value? They are ethical statements, after all, and Stevenson himself asserts that validity is a matter of truth. Stevenson would try to say that these statements have descriptive as well as emotive meaning, 'and that it is insofar as they express beliefs that the ordinary canons of logic apply to them'.[90] So we may use the first pattern of analysis to translate the argument as: I approve of anything that promotes liberty; education promotes liberty; therefore, I approve of education. All is well, the ethical statements having been interpreted descriptively. However, Wellman claims, now the major premise and conclusion are no longer ethical statements but factual statements about my attitude toward liberty. They do not establish the *attitude* expressed when I actually say, 'Liberty is good'. If, as Stevenson himself maintained, the point of ethical reasoning is to express one's attitude and change the attitudes of others, such moral arguments are useless.

I disagree. First, 'Liberty is good' could be translated not just in terms of first-person approval, but simply in terms of categorization, to aid our understanding – 'Liberty is one of the things of which I approve', 'X is good' could be translated descriptively as 'X is one of the things toward which I feel approval'.[91] Whether such a translation would result in a valid argument turns on the difference between syntactic and semantic validity. If we use the term 'valid' semantically (that is, if we understand validity in terms of the meaning of words), then Wellman is correct – Stevenson's emotivism does not allow valid moral arguments.[92] But if we use 'valid' syntactically (if we understand validity as a matter of grammar: form, structure and relation), we may speak quite comfortably of valid ethical arguments. Their validity is simply a matter of form. We could even try to squeeze them into elementary syllogisms. In fact, it is a simple matter to translate the liberty example into the formally valid form of *modus ponens*: If something promotes liberty, then that something is good; education promotes liberty; therefore, education is good. Valid? Yes. Sound? Perhaps not. Either way it is unenlightening.

Nonetheless, Stevenson would also urge us not to neglect the emotive meaning of the sentences used – it is the emotive meaning that gives them persuasive power. He could propose that the purpose of moral reasoning is twofold: insofar as moral sentences are descriptive, their purpose is to categorize their objects (perhaps as objects of approval or disapproval); insofar as they are emotive, their purpose is to persuade. The two are connected, perhaps, in that by categorizing the object attractively, the goal of persuasion will be aided. Persuasion itself does not need to qualify as valid or invalid, any more than do the rhetorical techniques upon which we all rely at present. We may speak of them as 'effective' or 'ineffective' at accomplishing their goals, but not 'valid' or 'invalid'. Insofar as moral sentences are emotive, then, logic is irrelevant.

On to another objection. Brand Blanshard claims that emotivism 'would require us to abandon ways of thinking which are far better grounded than it is itself'.[93] His first criticism, related to that point, is that 'emotivism is irreconcilable with our way of thinking of past or future values'.[94] For example, according to emotivism, if I say 'The suffering of slaves in the United States before the Civil War was bad', I am expressing a present attitude or feeling. Although such suffering occurred, I cannot say anything about it now that could have belonged to such suffering when it occurred, since my attitude toward it did not exist at that time. Thus, on Blanshard's interpretation, 'nothing bad has ever occurred, or at least it is meaningless to say that it has'.[95] This strikes him as absurd. The only way he can see for the emotivist to handle this problem is to assert that slaves had a negative attitude toward slavery at the time. But this would make ethical judgments into statements of fact, capable of truth or falsity, and emotivism would thus be false. So, 'if it adheres to the view that value statements express present feeling only, then it cannot consistently say that anything evil has ever happened, which is absurd. If it takes the natural way of avoiding this absurdity, it contradicts itself'.[96]

Yet Blanshard appears to have missed the point, for in emotivism it makes no sense at all to speak of an *event* as evil or bad. There is no property of evilness or badness residing in events, so *of course* nothing evil has ever happened. The judgment 'Suffering is bad' is the expression of an attitude toward suffering. Indeed, I would be expressing a present attitude toward the past suffering of slaves, but an emotivist could simply ask Blanshard how he could sensibly speak of my attitude *belonging* to the event when it occurred, even in a theory other than emotivism. What would it mean to say my attitude belonged to that suffering? If Blanshard is going to use this as a meaningful criticism, he needs to explain how a *thing* – be it an object or an event – could be bad, or evil. And he will need more to back it up than the vague impression that the alternative is absurd.

His second criticism charges that emotivism 'renders all our attitudes arbitrary and groundless'.[97] In a fit of gross oversimplification, he claims that emotivism divides our attitudes into the categories of favourable (expressed by 'good') and unfavourable (expressed by 'bad'). 'Now,' Blanshard writes, 'if we are asked why we take a pro-attitude toward something, we should no doubt answer that it is because of something good in the object which makes such an attitude appropriate.'[98] We favour the happiness of our children, and disfavour their unhappiness – that is, we call their happiness 'good', and their suffering 'bad'. Why? We would answer, Blanshard insists, that happiness is good and suffering is bad. Indeed we could, and likely would, answer in this way, but our tendency to do so establishes nothing.

Blanshard believes that 'It would be arbitrary and groundless to favor something if there was nothing good about it, or to disfavor it if there was nothing bad.'[99] And he seems to believe that our natural answer to the above question shows that we try to give reasons for our judgments. But all he's shown is that we're inclined to give bland and circular tautologies. He criticizes emotivism for leaving us with a world in which there 'is nothing good in enlightenment or happiness or dutifulness which can make it appropriate to favor them, nothing bad in pain or disease or death that could justify aversion to them'.[100] To him, such a view implies that we can never 'justify' our ethical judgments, all attitudes being equally groundless. He draws the absurd conclusion that the only routes open to emotivists are to either refrain from approving or disapproving of anything or to call everything good, 'since this is all that is needed to make it good in the only sense in which anything is so'. Not only does this not follow, but Blanshard reveals that he still does not get the point: to call something good is not to make it good, but to express a favourable attitude toward it. He insists on using the language and assumptions of another theory, which leads him to misunderstand *this* theory.

Perhaps Blanshard is trying to make a subtler point: our attitudes, if not based on features of their objects, would be completely arbitrary according to Stevenson's theory. In a sense, he may be correct. Does it matter? Stevenson would concede that our attitudes have causes, and these causes may include the attitudes and claims of others, memories associated with a given object, even our mood – all of these may cause us to have a certain attitude toward something. Perhaps I have a negative attitude toward loud noises because they hurt my ears. In this case, a feature of the object has given rise (at least in part) to that attitude. After all, none of our attitudes arises in a vacuum; each one has a cause, likely several. So, in the sense of 'random' or 'frivolous', our attitudes certainly are not arbitrary. Yet, in the sense of 'subjective', they are. So be it; Stevenson would admit that. Why does it matter? 'Of course we cannot justify our attitudes,' Stevenson might respond, 'and in that sense of course they are arbitrary. Nor can we justify our emotions and tastes and preferences. So what?'

At this point it seems that Stevenson's emotivism, if not Ayer's, is stronger than many have supposed. The most common objections, which we have hitherto considered, either fail entirely or do little but cast a small measure of doubt on some of Stevenson's claims. Although I do not accept emotivism, I find these criticisms utterly unconvincing. Our opposition to emotivism seems to be far more emotional than rational – I doubt we would accept the objections of Blanshard, Ross and Wellman if they were levelled against a theory that was not so alien to our 'philosophical sense'. However, the following objections strike me as much more effective. In the end, although we may not be able to refute emotivism conclusively, we find that it is at best weak, inadequate, incomplete and unconvincing.

First, Pigden contends that, because Ayer – and, for that matter, Stevenson – defines 'good' in terms of approval, and 'bad' in terms of disapproval, he is led into circularity.[101] If to approve of something is to feel that it is good or right (a natural, reasonable, interpretation), then 'Happiness is good' expresses the feeling that happiness is good. It has no content, emotive or otherwise. As definitions, mere tautologies get us nowhere. Thus, something more is needed.

Some of the most effective arguments against emotivism (Stevenson's version in particular, though they also apply to Ayer's) can be found in Toulmin's *An Examination of the Place of Reason in Ethics*. His general point is that emotivism is an inadequate theory because it cannot 'give an account of what is a good reason for an ethical judgment, or provide any standard for

criticising ethical reasoning'.[102] Stevenson, for instance, con-
centrates so exclusively on the meaning of ethical terms that he
utterly ignores their application – a mistake that in Toulmin's
opinion leads him to miss the very point of moral philosophy.
Many, perhaps most, of Toulmin's criticisms are not his original
creation, but he states them particularly well. He also brings to
mind some criticisms that we have already dismissed, but
approaches the debate from a more effective angle.

One reason emotivists are led astray, Toulmin claims, is their
assumption that because the test of accuracy used for moral
terms is sometimes self-referential (that is, based on one's own
attitude or state of mind: 'That's just how I feel!') it is *necessarily*
self-referential. It is not, so emotivism is misleading. He explains,
'if "good" and "right" were words for subjective reactions, the
answer to "Is this good?" and "Is this right?" could only be
"Well, I feel such-and-such a way about it" or "How can I tell
you how you feel about it? You should know!"'[103] We wouldn't
accept either of these as a complete answer to the question.

At that point, the objection seems poor, since we may have
inappropriate expectations. The objection's strength lies in our
ability to *conceive* of ethics in ways inconsistent with emotivism,
laying waste to its claim of self-referential necessity. We can, for
instance, conceive of everyone agreeing on a question of rightness 'in the sense of having the same standards or criteria of
goodness, of accepting the same reasons as good reasons for
their ethical judgments'.[104] The emotivisms of Ayer and Stevenson cannot make any sense of this fact because, in Toulmin's
view, they 'confuse the contingent difference in standards of
rightness and goodness (which there might not be) with the
logically necessary difference (which could not be otherwise) in
the standards of pleasantness, enjoyability and so on'.[105] They
equivocate between the moral and non-moral implications of
such words as 'value', and 'good'. Toulmin believes there are
significant differences between ethical value concepts and non-

ethical value concepts. Yes, he may be incorrect, but since he may be right (and since most people assume he is), emotivism must be able to explain its treatment of them as identical. The theories of Ayer and Stevenson need to provide a reason for us to treat what may very well be a contingent difference as a necessary difference, and what may not be self-referential as necessarily self-referential. The fact that we need not conceive of ethics as necessarily self-referential indicates that ethics is *not* necessarily self-referential. Neither Stevenson nor Ayer explains his assumption, and I do not see how they could.

By now we move to Toulmin's next criticism: emotivists have abstracted ethics so far away from its relationship to humanity that they've robbed it of much of its meaning and purpose. Stevenson, for instance, claims that if moral sentences do not have a truth-value, and if we still insist on speaking of moral arguments as valid or invalid, we ignore the fact that the question of a valid inference in ethics is now uninteresting. Ethical inferences are interesting only if they are capable of truth or validity (which, as we have seen, they may still be). Toulmin finds the claim outrageous, writing: 'Devoid of interest? If a man tells me that it is right for him to kick the niggers around, *because* everyone else does, is it of no interest whether his argument is valid or not?'[106] Emotivists may reply that by insistently focusing on validity in this case, we're just selecting the inferences that appeal to us most – leaving us with *two* paradoxes. 'For of course,' Toulmin writes:

> though you are doing that, you are not simply doing that – you are insisting, in addition, that his argument is really an invalid argument, that his reason is a bad reason and one which no one should accept. And similarly, in saying that any thing is good, you are of course saying that you approve of it (or at any rate would like to be able to approve of it), and that you want your hearer to approve of it also. But you are not simply doing

that – you are saying that it is really *worthy* of approval, that there really is a valid argument (a good reason) for saying that it is good, and so for approving of it, and for recommending others to do so too.[107]

Toulmin agrees that inferences to which we are psychologically disposed sometimes match 'inferences to which we ought to give assent'[108] – but the two are logically distinct. Again, this is not a conclusive refutation by any stretch. Ayer and Stevenson might simply reply that we believe such things because we wrongly believe in ethical facts. But these emotivists can give us no reason to believe their claim – and they cannot account for the beliefs just described. Toulmin, similarly, cannot give us a compelling reason to believe his claims either.

Nevertheless, a point raised, but not pursued, by Toulmin in that last criticism is that ethics deals with how we treat each other. One of the reasons we are so committed to our assumptions of ethical truth and knowledge is that we want to be able to say to someone, 'No, you can't torture me to death. Torture is wrong, because . . .' and then give reasons to prove that torture is wrong. Ethics is so intimately connected with our emotions, our well-being, our happiness and unhappiness, pain and pleasure, that we cannot accept that there is no truth to be found in it. Like Moore's intuitionism, emotivism is too cold and robotic to be of any use. Whereas Moore blithely ignored emotion, emotivism deals with it so abstractly that its significance is lost.

Perhaps there are no ethical facts inherent in things, no properties of goodness or badness. In other words, perhaps ethics is a social construction. But it does not thereby follow that there are no ethical facts to consider, facts which take our well-being into account. When he sets out his enlightened emotivism, Russell comes close to arguing that there *are* such ethical facts – despite the fact that moral judgments are optative, and despite the fact that there are no moral properties inherent in things.

The most powerful objection against Stevenson and Ayer is represented by the following example from Toulmin: Suppose I were to ask two people whether I should pocket the contents of a discovered wallet, or return the wallet to its owner. Which of these two courses of action should I follow? One person tells me I should follow the first course, not the second. Another tells me I should follow the second, not the first. 'They cannot both be correct,' Toulmin argues, 'for if they were I should be morally obliged to do the logically impossible – namely, to perform both of two mutually exclusive actions.'[109] But emotivism seems to allow both answers to be correct, since each respondent just feels differently about the available options.

Is he correct? The claim here is different from the claim that emotivism rules out disagreement, or dispute. We are dealing with *action*, with *behaviour*. And although many people use 'ought' without determining whether the recipient of their judgment is able to obey, when used effectively 'ought' implies 'can'. The strength of Toulmin's objection lies in the fact that an ethical theory, even as Ayer and Stevenson conceive of it, is supposed to clarify ethical concepts. Why? Because the purpose of an ethical theory is to help us use ethical concepts effectively – to communicate, to understand and, more importantly, *to judge, choose and act*.[110] Ethics is a practical matter. But emotivism, as Ayer and Stevenson formulate it, is impossible to apply. It is useless in moral decision-making.

Consider Toulmin's wallet example again. I find a wallet and am undecided as to whether I should return it to its owner or keep it for myself. Seeking moral guidance, I ask two people which course of action they would recommend. The first tells me to return the wallet to its owner. Why? 'Because', he tells me, 'that is the honest course of action and honesty is good.' What does that mean? No more than that my adviser approves of honesty. How does that help me? That second person tells me to keep the wallet and use the cash to buy myself a new jacket. Why?

'Because it is in your self-interest to do so, and acting in accordance with one's self-interest is good.' In other words, he approves of acting in accordance with self-interest. Again, so what? Both Ayer and Stevenson would interject, insisting on the importance of the persuasive aspect of moral judgment. Both of my advisers, they would say, will (or must) attempt to influence my attitude, to change my attitude to match theirs. Since they cannot offer any reasons, evidence, or arguments in *direct* support of their attitudes, the only path open to them is that of rhetoric – emotional, I would say manipulative, appeal. And the most effective, perhaps the only, way for these advisers to get me to share their attitudes is to convince me that those attitudes have a factual component of some sort. That is, they will be more successful in their goal of persuasion if they convince me that their attitude accords with some fact – that one should be favourably disposed toward honesty, for instance, because honesty is good, because there is something about honesty that makes it *worthy* of approval. Otherwise, I am unlikely to be persuaded to share the attitude.[111] The persuasive power of moral judgments seems to lie in our conviction *that they can be true.* This is why reasons, evidence and argument are given – to persuade the listener that a moral judgment is true. And this is why we have concepts of valid and invalid moral arguments. As Toulmin argues:

> Whenever we are faced with a number of courses of action, we shall have to choose between different sets of reasons for acting in the different ways, and between different arguments in support of the different possible decisions. If this is to be done at all methodically, we shall need to distinguish between those which are worthy of acceptance ('valid,' as we now call them) and those which are not worthy (or 'invalid').[112]

That need, he suggests, favours existing usage over emotivism's suggestions – for if an ethical theory is incapable of doing what an ethical theory is supposed to do, then it is inadequate.

At the very least, it seems to me *reasonable* to require a moral theory to meet the purposes of ethics before it can be accepted. That is, it must clarify the issues involved and explain all the relevant data and phenomena in such a way that it provides a basis for decision-making and judgment, and facilitates communication and understanding of ethical issues. One of the greatest strengths of Russell's later emotivism, we shall find, is that it manages to provide practical advice. It is useful. It can be applied. Ayer and Stevenson not only fail in this task, but shirk the responsibility entirely.

They fail, finally, because they do not even try.

Russell's Proto-Emotivism, 1913–22

The first public hints of Russell's gradual change from intuitionism to emotivism can be found in 'On Scientific Method in Philosophy', a paper delivered as the Herbert Spencer lecture at Oxford in the autumn of 1914. He has not obviously embraced emotivism at this point, but rather has come to accept a form of subjectivism, as well as a view of the psychological forces behind ethics different from anything with which Moore could feel comfortable. Russell, like so many twentieth-century ethicists, spent much of his time looking over his shoulder, hoping he had finally escaped Moore's arguments. A large part of the problem lay in the fact that, even though Russell had rejected Moore's objectivism, he continued to share many of Moore's assumptions. As Pigden notes, like Moore, 'Russell had long believed that you cannot derive an Ought from an Is (or more precisely, moral conclusions from non-moral premisses). [Now] he argues that it is illegitimate to derive an Is from an Ought or a non-moral conclusion from moral premisses.'[113] What one wishes to be the case – or believes *ought* to be the case – cannot be used to discover what truly is the case, and so a 'scientific' philosophy, one which aims at discovering what is true in the world, must eschew consideration of moral values.

Ethical values do not exist somewhere out there in the world, awaiting discovery. Rather, 'Human ethical notions . . . are essentially anthropocentric, and involve, when used in metaphysics, an attempt, however veiled, to legislate for the universe on the basis of the present desires of men.'[114] That is to say, we value ends which serve our purposes and desires. When, as in evolutionary biology and philosophy, we speak of the development of humanity from protozoans through primates as *progress*, we impose our subjective values on the universe – an unscientific habit that impedes the growth of our understanding. It 'makes man, with the hopes and ideals which he happens to have at the present moment, the centre of the universe and the interpreter of its supposed aims and purposes'.[115] Russell often understood ethics and politics as united in purpose: to impose one's desires upon society through persuasion or more sinister means.

Our values, then, are the product of our wishes and desires. They represent not facts about the world, but that which we wish was the case. By imposing these wishes on the universe, we deceive ourselves, and perhaps others, into believing that the objects of our wishes are objective facts. Indeed, the appearance of objectivity may be used to persuade others to share our desires.[116] We come to believe that the universe is teleological, that it has goals, and that those goals are similar to ours. On the other hand, 'The kernel of the scientific outlook is the refusal to regard our own desires, tastes and interests as affording a key to the understanding of the world',[117] as Russell so eloquently states in another article written around this time. If this is the case, if this is what it means to have 'a scientific outlook', and if moral values are the products of our wishes and desires, then certainly they can have no place in science. They cannot be used as part of the scientific project: a complete and accurate description of the world.

'Ethics', Russell writes, 'is essentially a product of the gregarious instinct, that is to say, of the instinct to co-operate with those who are to form our own group against those who belong to other groups.'[118] It is tribal, then, involving at least a tacit acknowledgment that those in our group generally tend to be good, and pursue 'desirable ends' – while those in other groups are generally evil, pursuing 'nefarious' ends. We are not usually conscious of our ethical subjectivity, believing, as explained above, that our ends are 'good' in some objective, universal sense. Then, 'When the animal has arrived at the dignity of the metaphysician, it invents ethics as the embodiment of its belief in the justice of its own herd.'[119] A rather Nietzschean sentiment from one who despised Nietzsche.

Russell's account makes room for the value of self-sacrifice, too, which typically arises only in regard to members of one's herd. In order to survive, we gregarious animals depend 'upon co-operation within the herd, and co-operation requires sacrifice . . . of . . . the interests of the individual. Hence arises a conflict of desires and instincts, since both self-preservation and the preservation of the herd are biological ends to the individual.'[120] In order for both ends to be achieved, all must be convinced of their mutual importance, and so, 'Ethics is in origin the art of recommending to others the sacrifices required for co-operation with oneself. Hence, by reflexion, it comes, through the operation of social justice, to recommend sacrifices by oneself, but all ethics [is] more or less subjective.'[121]

Russell does not wish to be taken as denying the significance of ethics. Although it lacks philosophical or scientific value, it has value in practice. To explain: 'What is valuable is the indication of some new way of feeling towards life and the world, some way of feeling by which our own existence can acquire more of the characteristics which we must deeply desire.'[122]

Nonetheless, this is of no importance to a scientific philosophy, one concerned with objective and universal facts.

The strength of Russell's argument, writes Pigden, depends on what he means when he claims that ethics is subjective. If he is offering simple subjectivism, in which 'X is good' means 'I approve of X', he runs into problems of which he had long been aware, problems discussed earlier in the present chapter.[123] Is this what Russell means to say? Pigden believes that, until 1935, 'it is not quite clear whether he was a subjectivist or an emotivist or whether he distinguished between the two positions'.[124] However, his use of 'wish' in connection with ethical sentences suggests that he might have meant 'I wish for more X' or, interpreted in the style of emotivism, 'Would there were more X'. If he means either of these, *conflict* and *dispute* are possible – though disagreement of opinion is not. Still, as an account of good, this is utterly inadequate, since it would entail that something cannot be good if we have it, or if everyone had it, or if we had enough of it. Whereas wishes definitely imply privation, 'good' does not.[125]

I expect that in the early stages of Russell's transition out of intuitionism he might have wavered between simple subjectivism and an emerging form of emotivism, unsure as to which was most convincing. Although Pigden claims that Russell's statements during this period make much more sense if we accept that he had already embraced a crude form of emotivism at this point, there really is nothing in these articles to directly indicate emotivism. I expect that Pigden wants to avoid labelling Russell a simple subjectivist. Still, although in 'On Scientific Method in Philosophy' his language is closer to that of simple subjectivism, his claim that values are products of wishes and desires indicates emotivism. For, if 'X is good' means 'I approve of X' then we appear to have an indirect *statement of* desire or wish. We are asserting that we have a certain desire or wish. If 'X is good' means 'I wish for X' or 'I desire X' an attitude is *implied*, though the sentence is an assertion. But if 'X is good' means 'Would that there were more X' then we have the expression of a desire. It seems more natural to speak of the latter as being the *product* of a desire or wish[126] than the former, especially since one's wishes and desires can be opposed to one's attitudes. One may have a favourable attitude toward something that one does not desire. I may approve of the practice of wearing lipstick without any desire to wear lipstick.

Then again, perhaps 'X is good' simply expresses approval. Russell simply does not clarify what he is trying to say, subtly inviting us to share in his confusion.

By the time he wrote on matters of practical ethics during the First World War, Russell's metaethical leanings had been clarified. In these practical articles he sounds more like an emotivist, so the claim that his emotivist tendencies were stronger than his simple subjectivist tendencies may be justified. In 'The Ethics of War', written in 1915, Russell's goal is to defend a weak form of pacifism as a general position, but along the way he clearly rejects the notion that moral judgments have truth-values, and rejects the idea that moral terms designate any properties, natural or not. He writes:

> Opinions on such a subject as war are the outcome of feeling rather than thought: given a man's emotional temperament, his convictions, both on war in general and on any particular war which may occur during his lifetime, can be predicted with tolerable certainty. The arguments used will merely reinforce what comes out of a man's nature. The fundamental facts in this as in all ethical questions are feelings; all that thought can do is clarify and harmonize the expression of those feelings.[127]

He has given us a glimpse of what he believes to be the dual role of practical ethics: the proselytization and clarification of one's own feelings (or attitudes). Russell intends to be persuasive, not necessarily enlightening.

Note the change in vocabulary. Now Russell refers to feelings instead of wishes and desires. He may include desires in the category of feelings – it is hard to pin him down on this point, for he tends to be sloppy with such terminology. But, in any case, wishes now appear to be excluded. He may also include attitudes in the category of feelings, or perhaps as the *products* of feelings. The two are certainly distinct, however, and once again one wishes he had spent some time clarifying their relationship.

That Russell regards his ethical sentences as products of emotion (or 'feelings') rather than reason is one thing – and at this point we should believe that he regarded them in this way – but one may be excused for wondering how he can then use facts and inductive arguments to support his moral position. It is on this point that Russell's old Harvard friend R.B. Perry pressed his attack, accusing him of inconsistency (not the last time he would meet that accusation), because Russell had argued that since human beings cannot reach a rational consensus on moral issues, when one makes a value judgment one is merely stating a preference – or perhaps a fact of personal taste. It is a terrible argument, since, as Pigden writes, 'we cannot arrive at a rational consensus on the causes and consequences of the Great War. Yet it does not follow that history and politics are matters of taste, however biased our judgments may be.'[128]

Russell, Perry charged, attempts to do more than simply express his emotions.[129] First of all, his arguments are hardly emotional – rather, they are dispassionate, even cold. Second, Russell attempts to support his moral claims with induction and experience. That being so, one need only attack this support to bring down Russell's moral claims; emotions are irrelevant and inconsequential. Third, throughout the article, Russell obviously believes that his moral claims are correct, that there is something true about them. Obviously, this implicit claim to truth is

incompatible with his theory.[130] Finally, Russell believes that
wars can be justified if they promote and preserve certain human
values – most obviously: life, liberty, happiness and intellectual
contemplation. He certainly appears, therefore, to believe that
values exist in some objective sense, so that war can be justified
only if these values are endangered. If not, what could he mean
by 'justification'?

Regarding Perry's first criticism, there is certainly no contradiction involved in a dispassionate expression of one's emotions.
We ran into this sort of criticism in our discussion of Ayer. As
Aiken writes: 'One can talk about one's feelings dispassionately;
but one can also express one's feelings without the expression
itself being "passionate". Feelings and their expression may be
those of a "disinterested spectator" or judge.'[131] One need not
rant hysterically to express one's emotions. Even so, we know
that, in his later moral and political work, Russell was sometimes
given over to passion. Not that it matters, really. The criticism is
silly – unless Perry can provide a clear standard by which the
expression of emotion can be accepted as the expression of
emotion.

Perry's second criticism is stronger. Russell agreed that statements of fact should be subject to conventional criticism, and
should be called true only when they endure steady criticism and
are supported by a body of evidence and argument. Does this
entail, however, that his moral judgments must be true or false to
the extent that they deal with factual matters? Russell did not
deal with this issue at any length during the war, but his later
writing makes it clear that he distinguished questions of fact
pertaining to ethics and questions of value pertaining to ethics
in a manner similar to Ayer. Aiken again: 'Russell would no
doubt say that the statement "This war led to unhappiness" is a
very different sort of statement than saying "War is bad and one
ought not go to war".'[132] Whereas the second statement is an
expression of attitude, the first is a statement of fact. The first

can be settled by an appeal to evidence, and is capable of truth or falsity. The second cannot. Russell, Ayer, and to an extent Stevenson, are united on this point.

Perry believes that happiness is the greatest good, and Russell usually appears to agree. But they disagree about both the means to that end and the status of statements regarding ends in general; Perry apparently believes ends can be empirically verified and Russell does not. To be sure, Russell uses evidence to support his views regarding the ethics of war – even when it comes to what are 'purely' ethical statements, not matters of fact related to ethics – but that, in itself, is not inconsistent with his emotivism. What matters, what makes the difference, is the *intention* behind the use of such evidence. Russell uses it to persuade, to convince others to share his emotions and attitudes toward the war, not to prove that 'war is wrong' is true. He is, in fact, using moral sentences the way both he and Stevenson believe they are properly used. The addition of evidence is an attempt to strengthen the persuasive appeal of his remarks. Years later, in *Religion and Science*, Russell would identify such tactics with the role of the preacher. 'He is only trying to change belief,' Aiken writes, 'and in so doing hoping that this change in belief will also causally change attitudes toward war.'[133]

Yet one cannot help but wonder what might happen if Russell thought the matter of persuasion through to its logical consequences. The role of the preacher or propagandist is essential, Russell believes, and he evinces approval of such work, which he had himself undertaken on many occasions. But how far can the preacher go in his attempts to persuade? After all, much of the persuasive power of ethical judgments is based on the illusion that they are true, as we have discussed. In order to keep the populace from sinking into amorality, and to keep himself in business, is the preacher justified in keeping the populace ignorant of the nature of moral judgments? Russell's theory appears to endorse such deceit if it would further our desires – if, for example, it would help us achieve lasting international peace. By 'justified', in fact, he sometimes appears to mean little more than 'effective in furthering our desires'. Deceit may be an effective means to a universally desired end. On the other hand, such manipulation certainly would interfere with our desire that the truth be told, which most of us seem to have, though we rarely express it. Although most of us, including Russell (as his frequent condemnations of dishonesty indicate) recoil at this sort of thinking, Russell's proto-emotivist theory does not seem to allow some means to be 'morally superior' than others. We will return to this issue in the next chapter.

Perry's third criticism is even more interesting. Russell claims that a war would be justified – that is, supported by compelling and relevant reasons – if it promoted and preserved human values. Exactly what is meant by 'human values' is unclear. If Russell is an emotivist at this stage, as he might be despite some subjectivist tendencies, we may take a human value to be something of which most people approve. Now if, Perry claims, one could persuade Russell through the presentation of facts and arguments that a given war will tend to this end, Russell must accept the conclusion that the war is justified. However, although Russell must change his belief about the war, it does not follow that he must also change his attitude. Beliefs and attitudes are not necessarily connected, at least not logically. If we accept Russell's theory, then, he could agree with all the facts, and believe that the war was justified, yet still say it was wrong. Is this not contradictory? I agree with Perry that it might be contradictory – if 'justified' is equivalent to 'good'. I am not certain, however, that Russell would equate the two. And if he does not, there is no contradiction, for a bad war may be justified as a 'necessary evil'. Do we have any reason to believe that 'justified' means the same thing as 'good'? To Russell at this stage, to call something 'good' is to approve of it. But to call something 'justified' is to say that it is an effective means to an end.

Justification *may* contain an element of approval, but there is something more. Most of us have probably been forced, on at least one occasion, to grudgingly admit that some act or argument of which we disapprove is, in fact, justified.

Responding to this criticism in 'War and Non-Resistance', Russell admits that he backs up his moral judgments with reasons, 'But all that can be proved in this way is that the opinion one is combating is by no means certainly true, and . . . the opinion one is advocating has as much in its favour as that of one's opponents.'[134] If ethical judgments were rational, we would be able to decide rationally what ought to be the case, and determine how it could be realized. However, in debates over ends, 'no argument is possible', since we have nothing but competing feelings or desires: 'If, for example, one man thinks vindictive punishment desirable in itself, apart from any reformatory or deterrent effects, while another man thinks it undesirable in itself, it is impossible to bring any arguments in support of either side.'[135] In an ethical debate over ends, neither side can *logically* support its case with argument, though Russell allows argument to have causal and persuasive roles. Factual arguments lend causal and persuasive support to a moral conclusion, used to persuade others that one's argument has better causal support than that of one's opponents; as Aiken states it: 'His view has so much in its "favour" that, granting his facts, others may perhaps change their attitudes to agree with his own.'[136]

On the other hand, when there is agreement on ends, but disagreement as to means, 'the difficulty is just the opposite: so many arguments can be brought on both sides of the question that no rational decision is possible'.[137] That is, all parties can keep bringing in new arguments at each level, down to the level of basic axiomatic ascriptions. At this point even science is useless – there are no more arguments, there is no more evidence, to consider. In the end, with a wealth of competing and contradictory arguments confusing the debate, we will accord weight to those arguments and facts which appear to support our feelings and attitudes toward the conclusion, and rationalize the others away.

That Russell could have responded by explaining the relationship between his arguments and his moral conclusions not as logical, but as causal, is significant. That is, the arguments may have caused, in whole or in part, the emotions Russell feels toward war. Since Russell never uses his facts and arguments to make his conclusions seem necessary, he is not inconsistent. In fact, emotivism cannot possibly rule out the use of argument in support of one's moral feelings, for even if facts and arguments can never justify such emotions, they may explain them. Like it or not, their existence is a psychological fact.

That said, Russell does want to appear rationally justified in 'The Ethics of War'. How can that be? He has run into the sort of problem Wellman identified in Stevenson's work. If he is an emotivist, then he is arguing without propositions much of the time – ethical statements do not appear capable of rational justification. How can they be used in arguments? Will Russell be forced to admit that there are no moral arguments, or are moral arguments different from other sorts of arguments? We will consider this issue in greater detail after we examine Russell's mature emotivism. He may be able to suggest, as Ayer and Stevenson did in their own ways, that the use of ethical sentences in arguments is admissible if they are used to categorize, or offer some sort of descriptive meaning. Better still, he may suggest adopting a syntactic understanding of validity.

The central point to remember, however, in defence of Russell's early subjectivism-cum-emotivism against Perry's criticisms, is that his arguments are intended to persuade readers to share his feelings and attitudes toward the First World War. Indeed, this may be the point of all moral arguments, as Stevenson believes.[138] As Aiken writes: 'The rest of Russell's arguments would be designed to change certain beliefs about the nature of the facts, thereby also changing attitudes.'[139] Reason may be used as a tool to clarify and systemize our emotions (as Russell claimed to be doing) to make us aware of connections we have not yet made between, for instance, causes and consequences. Rational argument can also be used to reinforce the convictions and emotions we already possess, as reassurance that we are justified in feeling as we do (even if justification, ultimately, is impossible). Russell did succeed in changing and clarifying the attitudes of some; 'his popular writings were . . . widely influential in helping to reach the kind of liberal, left-leaning political culture that has been the source of much that has been most humane in the twentieth century'.[140] Miles Malleson, who snuck into the back of a hall in which Russell was lecturing on the war, felt uneasy about losing many of his friends in battle. Confused and despairing, he heard Russell give 'a passionate and reasoned argument that this slaughter of my generation should be brought to an end as soon as possible. . . . I think that afternoon probably was a turning point in my own attitudes and thoughts about the world.'[141]

Thus it is possible, in fact simple, to adhere to an emotivist metaethics without abandoning moral activism. We may believe moral judgments are nothing more than expressions of emotions without feeling forced to keep our mouths shut on moral matters. Although Russell doesn't make this point explicit, Aiken notes, 'If this were not the case I doubt very much whether Russell would ever have written his article.'[142] Indeed, this fact fits in nicely with Russell's conviction that, in Monk's words, 'a stable peace can only be attained by a process of popular education and by a gradual change in the standards of value accepted by men who are considered to be civilised'.[143]

The problem, to many, is that Russell's emotivism at this stage contains no element of command, no imperative. He may speak out on moral issues, but why should anyone listen? We run into this problem with his mature emotivism as well.

As Pigden writes, Russell's practical ethics was informed by his normative ethics, his idiosyncratic rule-consequentialism. And his consequentialism is not necessarily in conflict with his emotivism. For, regardless of whether moral judgments are true or false, it may still be a matter of fact whether an action will maximize what one labels as good, or minimize what one labels as evil. Therefore, a moral judgment, in this naturalistic sense, can still be objectively true or false. Russell recognized this and, in *Religion and Science*, revealed that in his opinion it made such ethical matters a scientific pursuit, not a philosophical one.[144] Nonetheless, we still face a problem that both Ayer and Stevenson attempted to deal with. Even if moral judgments are capable of truth and falsity in the above sense, they will have power only over those who share one's ends. If I say that 'interpretive dance is good', and mean by good that it leads to a great balance of happiness over unhappiness, my judgment will matter only to those who wish to maximize happiness, who share my conception of good. So how do we persuade those who hold a different conception of moral good to share our conception? Russell denies that facts will be effective in such a circumstance. We are left with rhetoric – *preaching*, as Russell puts it – not philosophy. The ethicist must at this point become a moralist, excluding rationality from ethics at this level and assenting to the methods of rhetoricians, propagandists and clergy. And, perhaps, secular activists.

Russell wished to replace false beliefs in ethical objectivity and intrinsic values with a moral philosophy that stressed the cultivation of compossible or universalizable desires. Although he did not develop this goal until later, I believe his purpose is clear (if unexpressed) even at this stage. Denton interprets Russell as believing that, 'If ethics was only an expression of desire . . . then there was no reason to assume that any group of individuals, much less an entire society, would share equivalent desires, thereby rendering a social ethics by consensus impossible.'[145] I doubt, in fact, that Russell would agree with him. For one, the possession of ethical knowledge or truth does not make consensus likely unless we realize we share such knowledge, are able to separate this knowledge from our false beliefs, and are able to reconcile such knowledge with our desires. It may be the case that, even if we had certain ethical knowledge, it would be contrary to our desires. We could take science as an example of an area of life in which, although there is knowledge and truth, desires conflict. For Russell, this is a matter of human nature. He adheres quite fiercely to a sort of psychological egoism, believing that people desire similar things, primarily their own advancement and fulfillment. That we have similar desires does not lead us *out* of conflict, quite the opposite.

Denton offers a criticism which, I find, is far more compelling than the misinterpretation we have just discussed. Russell, recall, wishes to convince people to cultivate universalizable desires. Denton writes: 'If values have no intrinsic character . . . then they are rendered impotent by the political and economic conditions that shape the desires of different groups in society. Russell might call for the cultivation of "large and generous desires," ' but he may as well have been whistling in the wind.[146] Denton has a good point, but how might Russell respond? First, by pointing out that all of us, or at least nearly all of us, share certain desires and concerns, regardless of political, social or economic conditions. Primary among these is the desire for our own well-being, interpreted perhaps as the maximization of our own pleasure, happiness or satisfaction of our needs. We may appeal to such concerns, convincing people to listen because *their own* interests are at stake. If we wish to lead nations to peace, we can explain to them the probable consequences of war, hoping that by appealing to mutual self-interest, a recognition of overwhelmingly negative consequences will lead to peace.

Yet our shared desires and concerns may still lead us into conflict, as Russell's psychological egoism suggests. For, we may share a desire for a promotion. But if there is only one promotion to be awarded, my desire for it will conflict with yours. Russell's theory cannot offer a solution to this sort of problem.

A Parade of Failure

We have encountered a few criticisms of Russell's early theory – his proto-emotivism. Now we wish to know how it fares against its rivals. Is it a more plausible theory than the theories of Ayer and Stevenson? Does it survive the criticisms that maim those other theories?

Ayer's emotivism may be dismissed because of its reliance on the obviously false verification principle. Does Russell fall prey as well? He clearly rejects the possibility of empirical confirmation and observation in regard to ethical values (ends), but whether he rejects the possibility of analytic ethical sentences is unclear. Most importantly, he does not state, at this point, that the only meaningful sentences are either empirically testable or analytic.

When it comes to the weaker criticisms and objections levelled against Ayer and Stevenson (those of Ross, Wellman and Blanshard), Russell's theory fares rather well. Most of those dealt with the adequacy of emotivism's treatment of moral argument and dispute, and on the very point of using moral judgments. Some argued that, if moral judgments were merely expressions of attitude, no argument, dispute, and/or contradiction would be possible – formal logic would not even apply. Others argued that there would be no point to moral disputes if ethical judgments were not capable of truth and falsity.

Russell plainly believed that, whether ethical judgments are capable of truth or not, there was still a point to moral dispute. Like Stevenson and Ayer, Russell believed, at this stage, that one of the purposes of moral dispute was persuasion. We may dispute and argue in the hope of convincing our adversary to share our attitudes. Russell has no difficulty accepting the claim that, in a moral dispute, we become preachers or proselytizers, using rhetoric and other persuasive methods to propagate our attitudes. Some of us may find this distasteful, but Russell apparently does not.

When it comes to the possibility of contradiction and dispute, it is obvious that Russell believes such things are possible. Like Ayer and Stevenson, he accepted a descriptive meaning for ethical terms and judgments. When understood in that sense, two ethical sentences may contradict one another if they claim that a given action belongs in two opposed categories.

The stronger criticisms are more interesting, and Russell's ability to meet them is less obvious. What about Pigden's claim that Ayer and Stevenson are led into circularity? Their definitions in terms of approval led to useless tautologies. If we interpret Russell's definition of 'X is good' as 'I approve of X' it leads to the same sort of tautology. But if we interpret it as 'Would there were more X', Russell sidesteps the trap. Whether the first or second interpretation is correct is unclear. But if he was an emotivist, not a simple subjectivist, the second is likelier.

Toulmin criticized Ayer's and Stevenson's theories as inadequate because they provided no basis for distinguishing a good reason from a bad one in ethics, thus leaving us without any standard for criticism. Russell is able, at the very least, to say that a good reason for acting in one way over another is that it will help you achieve your goals (what he appears to mean by 'justification'). When it comes to means, his theory allows him to distinguish good reasons from bad on the basis of whether the action will lead to the desired end. Although nothing in Ayer's and Stevenson's theories prevents them from making the same claim, only Russell makes it explicitly. His recognition of good and bad reasons in the means also allows him to escape

Toulmin's claim that emotivism permits one to be obliged to do the logically impossible. Leaving aside the questionable assumption that one can be obliged by any received advice, Russell could say that the path one should take in such a situation is that which is more likely to lead to one's ends. In the wallet example, Russell's response might be to ignore any advice and do that which is most conducive to your own ends, in accordance with your own desires. But the case supposes that one is undecided. If so, Russell's theory appears to be of no more help in enabling one make a moral decision than Ayer's or Stevenson's. The criticism appears to apply to all three philosophers.

Similarly, the objection that emotivism is not necessarily self-referential applies to Russell as well. In fact, one could also argue that not only has Russell failed to provide any reason to believe that ethics is necessarily self-referential, his proto-emotivism does not even follow necessarily from his *a priori* anthropology of the origin of ethics. Russell was prone to such moral genealogies and histories (they precede and weave in and out of each attempt to explain his enlightened emotivism as well). Interesting as they may be, they often lack any necessary connection to his metaethical theories.

Yet when it comes to the purpose of ethical theory, and the charge that emotivists abstract ethics to such a degree that they miss the forest for the trees, ignoring the very purpose of ethics, Russell stands apart from his fellow emotivists. Matters of practical ethics occupy his mind consistently during this period – and indeed, throughout the rest of his life. He is obviously concerned with ethical decision-making. Some used this concern to attack his emotivism, accusing him of inconsistency. As long as everything is carefully (one might say sophistically) interpreted, he is able to avoid charges of inconsistency, though his emotivism may not be the glorious force for good he sought. Nonetheless, of all the criticisms levelled at Ayer and Stevenson, this is the one Russell clearly, unequivocally, avoids. His intellectual curiosity about ethical matters was always accompanied by intense concern for the issues at hand and the people involved. Obviously, then, Russell did attempt to make his theory relevant to the concerns of human beings – he recognized the intimate connection between ethics and human needs. But he failed to provide a theory capable of providing us with any reliable guidance, standards for judgment, or means for making decisions and solving disputes, unless we count his inadequate conception of justification.

The fact that Russell spends most of his time at this stage applying his theory might explain why he spent so little time *explaining* it. His proto-emotivism is a muddle, a confused and confusing mess of a theory, if we can call it a theory at all. Extracting a theory from the fragments he offers is a difficult task. Indeed, we may be creating it for him, since it is not at all clear whether he had an actual 'theory' at this stage. Comparing Russell's early 'theory' to Ayer's and Stevenson's is thus little more than a guessing game, since we cannot even be certain what he takes 'X is good' to mean.

What can we conclude? Russell's proto-emotivism appears to be marginally superior to those of Ayer and Stevenson, but it also faces new problems – in part because of Russell's commitment to practical ethics and moralizing. Still, his work at this stage is rather frustrating. He appears to be blissfully unaware of the implications and ramifications of his position, to the extent that he has one. Worse still, he does not bother to present a worthwhile argument on its behalf, leaving later apologists to reinterpret and fill in the blanks. Ayer and Stevenson, despite their many faults, at least presented fairly complete, largely coherent, arguments for their theories. Russell's theory appears in confusing bits and pieces.

On the other hand, we will find in the next chapters that Russell is able to develop, modify and formulate his theory in such a way that many of the problems we have discussed no longer apply. Whereas Ayer and Stevenson were forced to defend their theories in unconvincing ways, Russell's later version is actually somewhat compelling.

Notes

1. Mary Warnock, *Ethics Since 1900*, 2nd edition (London: Oxford University Press, 1966), 56–7.
2. Alfred Jules Ayer, *Language, Truth and Logic*, 2nd edition (New York: Dover Publications, Inc., 1946), 102–3; henceforth 'Ayer, *LTL*'.
3. Precisely what constitutes an 'ethical' concept (or term – the two are not equivalent, though sometimes Ayer appears to have them confused) as opposed to a non-ethical one is unclear. Ayer is entirely unhelpful on this point, though going by remarks later in his chapter on ethics and theology, I expect he includes such concepts as 'goodness', 'badness', 'rightness' and 'wrongness' – in at least some of their uses. Surely, many of the concepts he classifies as non-ethical will be considered ethical by some. And it is probably the case that some concepts are both ethical and non-ethical, depending on context. If this is the case, it makes little sense to deride philosophers for including 'non-ethical concepts', unless Ayer can provide clear criteria for distinguishing them from ethical concepts, and from concepts that straddle the border. He also assumes a very strict demarcation of 'fact' from 'value' – an assumption that, in this case especially, deserves clear explanation.
4. Ayer, *LTL*, 103.
5. Ibid. You will be forgiven for furrowing your brow at that remark. Still, Ayer is merely giving expression to a view common in his day, that philosophy is a second-order discipline. Stevenson, we should note, also believed that the role of moral philosophy was to analyze ethical terms. Though this sort of view is usually associated with the positivists, others (perhaps we could say those on the periphery of positivism) held it as well.
6. Ibid., 103–4.
7. According to the verification principle, however, the fourth set of sentences must be 'strictly meaningless' (in a literal sense).

8. In *Ethics and Language* (1945), Stevenson elaborated on the arguments set forth in the article I am using in painstaking detail. Aside from this book, the most significant of his further elaborations, clarifications, additions and revisions are to be found in *Facts and Values* (1963), 'Persuasive Definitions', and 'Ethical Judgments and Avoidability' (both 1938). Whether he accepted the verification principle is not obvious, but it would not have led him into any major contradictions. Nonetheless, whether he accepts it implicitly or not, that he does not *rely* on it is significant – for this feature alone makes his theory stronger than Ayer's.

9. C. L. Stevenson, 'The emotive meaning of ethical terms', *Readings in Ethical Theory*, 2nd edition, eds. Wilfrid Sellars and John Hospers (New York: Meredith Corporation, 1970), 254; henceforth 'Stevenson, EMET'.

10. Ibid., 254. Yes, the analogy is odd.

11. Ibid.

12. Ibid., 255.

13. Ibid.

14. Ibid., 256.

15. Ibid. I'd interpret this to mean, and Warnock appears to agree, *any* scientific method.

16. Ibid. By 'interest theories', Stevenson means moral theories which identify the good with attitudes, such as approval. In an interest theory, roughly, the Good is that toward which an individual or society feels an emotion of approval.

17. Ibid.

18. Ibid., 256–7.

19. Ibid., 257. Or it might suggest that we are missing the point.

20. Ibid. Throughout this book I will substitute 'attitude' for 'interest', as Stevenson uses the term in an old-fashioned and somewhat idiosyncratic manner. What he means by it corresponds to what we now tend to mean by 'attitude'.

21. Ayer, *LTL*, 105.

22. Ibid.

23. Stevenson, EMET, 259.

24. Ibid.

25. Ayer, *LTL*, 108.

26. Stevenson, EMET, 257.

27. Ibid. The example I have used is a modification of that used by Stevenson.

28. Ibid., 258.
29. Ibid. Highly suggestive of Richard Dawkins' and Daniel Dennett's speculations regarding the transmission of 'memes'.
30. Ayer, *LTL*, 107.
31. Ibid. Stevenson, note, does not mean to suggest that ethical concepts are 'pseudo-concepts', only that they are not empirical.
32. Warnock, *Ethics Since 1900*, 58. Note that throughout their work, Ayer, Stevenson and Russell assume the truth of Moore's claim that the Good cannot be a natural quality. It may be, it may not be. But they assume it without any argument or discussion. I doubt very much that the emotivist project would ever have taken off as it did had the emotivists not felt such tremendous respect for Moore's work.
33. Precisely why he considers this rare is unclear. He gives no reason, and the more natural assumption is that assertion without expression is quite common. Not everyone reacts to moral transgressions with, say, expressions of outrage. Some people make moral judgments so matter-of-factly that they betray no disposition at all regarding the act in question. One may say, truthfully, 'I find it difficult, even impossible, to express my moral horror'. And Ayer's earlier admission that moral terms can be used descriptively allows for such a phenomenon. So why can we not postulate such descriptive moral 'judgments' as moral judgments *per se*? A better contrast may be, as Nicholas Griffin has suggested to me, between description and exhibition. In that case, emotivism could be characterized as 'exhibition ethics'.
34. Sir David Ross, 'Critique of Ayer', *Readings in Ethical Theory*, Sellars and Hospers, 251.
35. If we were to try defining a term, we would of course try to take all of its meanings into account, find the common factors, and make them explicit.
36. Even those who will not allow that a great number of people can be wrong about the meaning of a word will, I expect, grant that a great number could be mistaken about matters of objectivity and truth-value.
37. Warnock, *Ethics Since 1900*, 67.
38. Stevenson, EMET, 259.
39. Ibid., 260.
40. Ibid., footnote 6. I here use, following Warnock, the reformulated conception of emotive meaning found in *Ethics and Language*, which

Stevenson placed in a footnote in the reprinted version of EMET.
Note the wordiness characteristic of that book.

41. Ibid., 261.
42. Ibid.
43. Ibid. He is uncomfortable translating it as 'we like X', but cannot find a better phrase. He hopes the rest of his discussion will clarify what he means.
44. Although this may seem to contradict its third use, that is not necessarily the case.
45. Ibid., 262.
46. Ibid.
47. Ibid.
48. Ibid.
49. Even he does not call it a definition, in a strict sense of the word.
50. Ibid., 263.
51. Ibid.
52. Ibid., 263–4.
53. Warnock, *Ethics Since 1900*, 69.
54. Stevenson, EMET, 264.
55. Ibid.
56. Ibid., 265. That persuasion and manipulation are necessary conditions of personal growth may be questionable.
57. Ayer, *LTL*, 107–8.
58. Ibid., 110. Ayer's phrasing of the objection is somewhat irritating, since it refers to *statements about* the speaker's emotions, not expressions of them – so it would not be an objection to emotivism at all. Still, the analogous point is clear in his subsequent remarks.
59. Ibid., 111.
60. Ibid. Although we sometimes say such things as 'You shouldn't feel that way', or 'Don't you know how much your anger bothers others?', these pleas may be useless. In most circumstances, it seems obvious that people cannot control how they feel – that at best they can pro-actively try to *prevent* some emotions. So we could reasonably advise people to learn how to prevent, say, angry outbursts. But chiding someone for *being* angry strikes me as pointless.
61. Ibid.
62. Ibid. Russell, we will discover, tends to sympathize with Ayer on this point, but Stevenson disagrees.
63. Ibid., 21.
64. Ibid. Thanks to Nick Griffin for the new term!

65. Ibid.
66. Ibid.
67. Ibid., 22.
68. Ibid.
69. This appears to be the case in ethics, yes, but in everything else as well. Recall Russell's unease with the axioms of Euclidean geometry. At some point, reasons must come to an end. I lean toward some form of foundationalism in believing that some beliefs, propositions, principles and so forth must be taken as properly basic – such as the law of non-contradiction.
70. Ross, 'Critique of Ayer', 251.
71. I am aware that a dispute is not necessarily identical with a difference of opinion, but will ignore that issue here.
72. Pigden, *RoE*, 133.
73. An interesting suggestion from Sami Najm is: 'Two attitudes contradict each other if one cannot have both and still be sane.'
74. Carl Wellman, 'Emotivism and ethical objectivity', Sellars and Hospers, *Readings in Ethical Theory*, 285. Italics added.
75. Let us say that two attitudes are (strongly) incompossible in the following sort of situation: I approve of everyone's approving of X, and my adversary approves of everyone's disapproving of X. Thus, our attitudes are not only incompatible, but they cannot both be satisfied, and are bound to lead to a conflict between us. (Thanks to Nick Griffin for his suggestions.)
76. Wellman, 'Emotivism . . .', 285.
77. Ibid.
78. Ibid., 285–6.
79. Ibid., 286.
80. Ibid.
81. Although Stevenson spends a fair amount of time discussing the *primacy of persuasion* in the use of ethical terms ('good') and sentences ('X is good'), note that he sometimes neglects to include this role in his attempts to define 'good'. Such carelessness may have contributed to Wellman's confusion.
82. Although, so long as my adversary does not *act* on her attitude, I may find her amusing.
83. Wellman, 'Emotivism . . .', 276.
84. Ibid., 280.
85. Ibid., 282. The argument is found in C. L. Stevenson, *Facts and*

Values: Studies in Ethical Analysis (New Haven: Yale University Press, 1963), 216–7.

86. Wellman, 'Emotivism . . .', 282–3.
87. As a whole Ayer claims that ethical sentences are not 'strictly meaningful'. But insofar as they have a secondary descriptive meaning, even he would allow them to have some 'strict' meaning.
88. See Pigden, *RoE*, 133.
89. In C. L. Stevenson, *Ethics and Language* (New Haven: Yale University Press, 1944), 116. Stevenson, bless him, does not offer a clear statement of the first pattern of analysis. As distinguished from the second pattern, though, its purpose is to clarify the meaning of ethical terms 'by limiting their descriptive reference to the speaker's own attitudes' (ibid., 89). It is the sort of analysis Stevenson attempts in EMET.
90. Wellman, 'Emotivism . . . ', 280.
91. The descriptive meaning, in Stevenson's analysis, flirts with simple subjectivism.
92. Within the first pattern of analysis, at least.
93. Brand Blanshard, 'The impasse in ethics – and a way out', Sellars and Hospers, *Readings in Ethical Theory*, 294.
94. Ibid., 294–5.
95. Ibid., 295.
96. Ibid.
97. Ibid.
98. Ibid.
99. Ibid.
100. Ibid., 296.
101. Pigden, *RoE*, 132.
102. Stephen Toulmin, *An Examination of the Place of Reason in Ethics* (Cambridge: Cambridge University Press, 1950), 29.
103. Ibid., 34–5.
104. Ibid., 35.
105. Ibid. The difference in standards of pleasantness and enjoyability, etc., is logically necessary, Toulmin believes, because these things are *necessarily* self-referential, experiences being different for everyone. Rightness and wrongness are not – necessarily.
106. Ibid., 34. Emphasis added.
107. Ibid., 39.
108. Ibid., 39.
109. Ibid., 32. I would qualify the issue as one of being *advised* to do the logically impossible, for neither 'ought' nor 'should' necessarily implies obligation.

110. Perhaps this is why the most convincing metaethics seem to be tied to a normative theory.

111. I may, of course, be persuaded *to act as though* I share the attitude if I were shown that such behaviour would be in my self-interest.

112. Toulmin, *An Examination*, 41.

113. Pigden, *RoE*, 106.

114. Bertrand Russell, 'On scientific method in philosophy', *Mysticism and Logic*, 3rd edition (London: Unwin Books, 1963), 82; henceforth 'Russell, SM'. Russell's previous objectivist ethic, for example in 'A free man's worship', was an example of the projects he criticizes in this paper.

115. Russell, SM, 82.

116. As we have discussed, the appearance of objectivity may even be *necessary* for the moral persuasion of some people.

117. Bertrand Russell, 'The place of science in a liberal education', *Mysticism and Logic*, 37. If we interpret this as a characterization of objectivism in ethics, we could accuse Russell of misrepresentation. However, I doubt he is levelling a charge at any particular metaethical theory.

118. Russell, SM, 82.

119. Ibid.

120. Ibid.

121. Ibid.

122. Ibid., 83.

123. In particular, the problems faced by reducing moral judgments to sentences expressing one's psychological state – i.e. 'I approve of X'. It is interesting to note that Russell's early 'desire to desire' theory was a form of simple subjectivism, which he abandoned before coming under Moore's spell. That he sometimes seems to be leaning toward simple subjectivism at this stage may be a sign that he toyed with returning to his old theory once Moore's influence began to fade.

124. Pigden, *RoE*, 107.

125. Wishing for more of the Good in the future could imply an anxiety about possible privation, but this seems to imply that, say, pleasure is good only if we don't have it – that it is not good now, when I have it, but may be good once it is gone.

126. One wishes Russell had made his meaning clear. As a matter of charity we may wish to interpret his meaning as: 'X is good' is the product of a desire – since one can desire what one has, does not have, would like more of, would like more of in the future, and so on.

127. Bertrand Russell, 'The ethics of war', *Justice in Wartime*, 2nd edition, (London: George Allen & Unwin, Ltd., 1917), 19. I doubt whether such

an absolute disjunction between 'feeling' and 'thought' is possible, but it is an assumption common to Russell and his contemporaries.

128. Pigden, *RoE*, 111. Pigden's analogy may be flawed. If he means, by 'cannot', that it is not a practical possibility, the analogy holds. But if he is referring to logical (or even statistically insignificant) possibility, the analogy does not apply. In the case of ethics, Russell is probably referring to logical impossibility – in the case of The First World War, *practical* impossibility.

129. Perry's argument as found in Lillian W. Aiken, *Bertrand Russell's Philosophy of Morals* (New York: The Humanities Press IAC., 1963), 69; henceforth 'Aiken, *BRPM*'. Perry's article, 'Non-resistance and the present war' was published in the April 1915 issue of *The International Journal of Ethics*.

130. However, if we are all confused about what we are doing when making moral judgments, it should come as no surprise that Russell is confused as well!

131. Aiken, *BRPM*, 69. We must also distinguish between the description of an emotion and the expression of it. The former has a truth-value, whereas the latter does not.

132. Ibid., 70.

133. Ibid.

134. Pigden, *RoE*, 112.

135. Ibid.

136. Aiken, *BRPM*, 71.

137. Pigden, *RoE*, 112.

138. This may also be the point of all or most *non-moral* arguments.

139. Aiken, *BRPM*, 63.

140. Pigden, *RoE*, 4.

141. Quoted in Clark, *The Life of Bertrand Russell*, 279.

142. Aiken, *BRPM*, 64. Aiken also notes that Russell himself did not appear to distinguish between the expressive and persuasive functions of moral language.

143. Monk, *Bertrand Russell*, 372. Monk is using 'civilised' descriptively, in the manner in which Russell uses it. Obviously, it is nonetheless loaded with moral connotations.

144. Bertrand Russell, *Religion and Science* (Oxford: Oxford University Press, 1935), 228–9; henceforth 'Russell, *RS*'.

145. Peter H. Denton, *The ABC of Armageddon* (Albany: State University of New York Press, 2001), 108.

146. Ibid., 108.

3

Enlightened Emotivism

Achieving Enlightenment

Russell's mature emotivism finds a way to work by incorporating elements of the 'desire to desire' theory of his youth and backing this up with the work on desire begun during the First World War, primarily that found in *Principles of Social Reconstruction.* This 'enlightened emotivism' is much more sophisticated and nuanced than the theory he held earlier.[1] Not only is the mature theory more complex than its predecessor – and than the later theories of Ayer and Stevenson – it is far more convincing as well, enabling Russell to feel far more comfortable with his ethical paradigm shift than he had previously.

Although elements can be found in *What I Believe* and *Outline of Philosophy*, we find Russell's first overt declaration of sophisticated emotivism in *Religion and Science*, published in 1935 – two years after Barnes' 'A Suggestion About Value' and one year before Ayer's *Language, Truth and Logic*.[2] He appears to have chosen this book to come out of the emotivist closet because it is his call-to-arms against the popular belief that science alone is insufficient and must be supplemented by religion in the realm of value.[3] Here he admits that science has nothing to say about values, but denies that there is a realm of knowledge – ethical knowledge – inaccessible to science and open to religion. There is no ethical knowledge, Russell claims, because there is no ethical truth. As Ayer later argued, there is nothing to be known in ethical judgments, and so there is no extra-scientific moral realm containing facts beyond rational apprehension. Science 'is impotent' in matters of value. That is: 'Science can tell us much about the means for realizing our desires but it cannot say that one desire is preferable to another.'[4] Russell writes: 'Whatever knowledge is attainable, must be attained by scientific methods; and what science cannot discover, mankind cannot know.'[5]

Now Russell makes it quite clear that value judgments are not propositions – they are optative. Whereas his 'desire to desire' theory held that to say 'X is good' is to say "I desire to desire X", which is a *statement* of one's desire, capable of truth or falsity, he now claims it is an *expression* of a desire – namely, 'Would that everyone desired X.' Drawing on a distinction he first made in 1893, Russell insists that, in Pigden's words: 'The fact that the speaker desires everyone to desire X can be inferred from what the speaker says, but it is not part of what the speaker is saying.'[6] It will soon become apparent that despite the impossibility of truth or falsity, a measure of objectivity remains in this form of emotivism.

The Preacher and the Legislator

Our concept of good, Russell claims, arises from reflection on conflicting desires, both between different people and within the same person. Each of us is a hub of desires, some of which conflict with one another, some with the desires of others. Each desire is sometimes stronger, sometimes weaker – both in comparison to its earlier and later states and to other desires. Through reflection we realize that it is impractical to act upon whichever desire is at present stronger, as such rash actions may vanquish the chances of other desires that maintain a lower level of strength over a longer span of time (those concerned with long-term goals, for instance). As an example, one's desire for security may be weaker, most of the time, than many other desires. But it is long-term; that is, we always have it to some degree and we always will. If we were to act rashly on a powerful desire for vengeance, we could be led to ends that jeopardize our desire for security, and thus we will have satisfied a momentarily strong desire that fades quickly over a more significant long-term desire – 'significant' in that it allows us to achieve much more over a longer span of time.

Eventually, if we mature emotionally and intellectually, we come to desire a 'harmonious life, i.e. a life in which action is dominated by consistent quasi-permanent desires'.[7] Some desires are more likely to help us realize this goal than others, as the above example demonstrates. So the more rational among us resolve to give priority to significant, long-term desires that are compossible with a great many others.

Russell does not offer any argument for the contentious claim that a desire for a harmonious life is the inevitable outcome of maturity; he assumes we will find its truth obvious. Yet it is far from obvious. He assumes that 'mature' desires for a harmonious life of peace with oneself and one's neighbours are *better* than 'immature' desires – the labels are loaded, after all. Say, for example, that I desired a life of constant drunkenness, easy women and late-night drag races down crowded city streets before dying in a brilliant fireball at the age of thirty. We will all concede that these are immature desires. But on what basis can Russell claim that such desires are worth less than those we label 'mature'? On the face of it, his implicit claim that 'mature' desires are better precisely because they allow us to satisfy a greater number of desires than 'immature' desires seems acceptable. But it would be quite easy to live a harmonious life guided by 'mature' desires in which one experiences very little satisfaction – one could, for instance, lead a harmonious life as the result of having few desires to satisfy. Simple tastes and all that. On the other hand, the hard-drinking, fast-living lifestyle we're considering *may* allow one to satisfy thousands of strong desires in a short period of time. For someone brimming with such 'immature' desires, the 'harmonious' life that Russell emphasizes may actually prevent him from satisfying any of his desires – because those desires are incompatible with the 'harmonious' way of life. The quiet life of the stereotypical tax accountant permits the satisfaction of different sorts of desires than the wild life of a spoiled yuppie anarchist. So on what basis can Russell justify demeaning the latter lifestyle in favour of the former?

Russell wants to avoid ranking desires in terms of their strength – the intensity with which one feels them – because he understands that the strongest desires are often the most destructive. Yet desires based on love and curiosity can also be quite strong, so he may be throwing out the baby with the bathwater. He clearly ranks desires (as his use of 'mature' and 'rational' indicates), but it is not immediately clear how he can justify the practice. For one, he must be able to define 'mature' and 'rational' in non-evaluative terms or find a way to justify their clearly evaluative use from within emotivism. Second, his theory appears to forbid any 'objective' ranking of desires – 'X is a better desire than Y' means 'Would that everyone desired X instead of Y.' What can he do?

The secret lies in the emotivists' old friend, compossibility. Albert's desire is compossible with Bertha's if both can be satisfied, otherwise the desires are incompossible. Within Albert, *desire X is compossible with desire Y if both X and Y can be satisfied,* otherwise they are incompossible. Compossibility is a simple concept, and a necessary one for any practical application of emotivism. Russell can use it to justify calling 'mature' desires better than 'immature' desires because the former are compossible with the desires of others whereas the latter are not. In fact, he seems to have something like this in mind as a criterion for distinguishing 'mature' from 'immature' desires: 'mature' desires are those that are compossible with the greatest possible number of other desires (or perhaps, in a weaker sense, *many* desires). 'Immature' desires, then, are incompossible with most other desires by definition. It may be that neither of two conflicting desires is compossible with very many other desires, but in that case, Russell could tell us to choose the lesser of two 'evils'. What matters, though, is that Russell can use this concept to rank desires: those desires that are compossible with the greatest number of other desires are the best, and those that are incompossible with the greatest number of desires are the worst. The rest, the bulk, fall somewhere in between. Thus, Russell may avoid using the strength of desires to rank them, and his ranking is consistent with his emotivism, for it makes good sense to call a desire at the top of the hierarchy 'good' if by doing so you are expressing the desire that everyone desire it. Of *course* you would – if only because it is ultimately to your advantage.

Where our 'wild lifestyle' objection fails is in its assumption that the only desires to be taken into account are one's own. While Russell certainly believes that our own desires are worth no less than those of others, he does not believe they are worth more, as we will discuss in greater detail momentarily.

But what about Russell's *evaluative* use of the terms 'mature' and 'rational'? Can he justify his use of these terms from within emotivism? He could probably do so through stipulative definition in the case of 'mature', although (as with all stipulative definitions) the results would be somewhat arbitrary and circular, taking advantage of popular connotations of the words in order to draw people into accepting the conclusions he wishes them to accept. He could, for instance, define 'mature' as 'fully developed and reasoned, and/or cautious and considerate' – thus taking into account a variety of meanings that the word has in popular usage.[8] His use of the word would still be controversial, but we could understand how Russell, as an emotivist, could use the word sensibly. A 'mature' desire, then, would be one to which we have given careful thought, the consequences of its satisfaction having been rationally anticipated and found compossible with the satisfaction of other desires within and without. A mature desire is *universalizable* as well, in that we can reasonably say of it, 'Would that everyone desired X.' As for 'rational', Russell need not use the word evaluatively – though it will always have evaluative connotations, positive or negative, to most people. By 'rational people' he could mean, simply: 'Those who attempt to decide according to a careful analysis of the probable consequences of each course of action, and who resolve, after such analysis, to take that course of action which is supported by a balance of positive (desired) over negative (not desired) reasons.' Again, we will never escape controversy with such a definition, but we can at least understand his use of the term.

We may accept his implicit claim that reason can adjudicate among desires by leading us to understand that certain desires allow us to satisfy more of our goals, and it is thus rational to indulge those desires over others. Since we 'mature' people probably desire the satisfaction of as many of our desires as possible, the rational conclusion ('You should indulge desire X instead of desire Y') would not lead to conflict. It *might* lead to conflict with the desires of the immature majority, but Russell does not discuss how such a conflict might be resolved. Presumably, if we were dealing with others whose immature, short-sighted, desires conflicted with the rational conclusion, Russell would suggest reasoning with them, trying to persuade them that indulging desire X instead of desire Y is in their own best interests. But if the desire is strong enough, such reasoning would have no effect, as Russell recognized. On the other hand, if we were dealing with an internal conflict of reason versus short-sighted desire, what could be done? I doubt such a conflict would even arise. A strong desire would simply overpower reason. Instant resolution.

One might ask whether such a resolution would be the *best*

resolution. Is it vulnerable to criticism? Can it be justified? How could Russell make sense of justification and criticism in this context? I will postpone discussion of these questions until we reach Russell's criteria of the 'good life'.

Russell recognizes that conflicts of desire *between different people* are more difficult to resolve. In settling such disputes, Russell claims, we must distinguish between the point of view of a disinterested authority who may settle the dispute, and the points of view of the actual disputants. More importantly, we must distinguish 'between what we wish people to *do*, and what we wish them to *feel* in the way of emotions and desires'.[9] Obviously, 'there will be a greater *total* satisfaction when two people's desires harmonise than when they conflict, but that is not an argument which can be used to people who in fact hate each other'.[10] From the point of view of a neutral authority, all the desires of all people, individually and in themselves, are equal – we have no reason to prefer the satisfaction of Albert's desires to Bertha's. Yet if we consider desires as a collective, we find that:

> sometimes all the desires in a group can be satisfied, whereas in other cases the satisfaction of some of the desires in the group is incompatible with that of others. If A and B desire to marry each other, both can have what they want, but if they desire to kill each other, at most one can succeed . . . Therefore the former pair of desires is socially preferable to the latter.[11]

Pragmatically, Russell makes a lot of sense thus far.

If ethics is meant to identify certain of our desires as more significant than others (because they lead to greater satisfaction), and promote them, how do we go about this? We have two methods: 'the way of the legislator' and 'the way of the preacher'. The impartial, objective, and disinterested legislator deals with 'what we wish people to *do*'. He or she attempts to create a moral code, a set of laws, that will promote conduct expected to maximize interpersonal ends – that is, social ends that will facilitate the satisfaction of citizens' compossible desires. If one allows personal desires to influence the creation of a moral code, one has failed to conform to the basic requirement of such a code – for we are looking for 'attitudes which will embody *impersonal* moral rules'.[12] A code devised this way will, following Russell's utilitarian assumptions, prescribe ends agreeable to the greatest number of people.[13] It is a manifestation of 'social conscience', connected to a system of education that will cause those who disobey it, who pursue ends contrary to those set forth by the legislator, to feel 'wicked'.[14] Consequently, ' "virtue" will come to be in fact, though not in subjective estimation, subservience to the desires of the legislator in so far as he himself considers those desires worthy to be universalized.'[15] In submitting to the rule of this *ideal* legislator, one is supposedly acting according to the interests of individual conscience. The laws are the real authority, not the legislator, and the authority behind those laws is the community.[16]

Is it possible to find such an impartial legislator? Since the laws depend on what the legislator deems 'worthy' to be universalized, there is obviously vast potential for abuse – which we might attempt to prevent by ensuring that the legislator is not one person, but a committee, or society itself (a collection of institutions, laws and leaders). Given the plainly horrifying consequences of legislating morality that we find throughout history, we had best ensure that the legislator (be it one or many) has a firm understanding of which desires truly are universalizable. And real legislators fall short of the ideal.

A larger problem is that under the legislator virtue seems to be identified with obedience, i.e. subservience to the legislator's supposedly benevolent will – a view of virtue that Russell despises. Yes, the authority behind the laws may, ultimately, be the community that decides to follow them, but this is nonetheless an ethics of obedience, justified by an appeal to authority. Russell forcefully rejects authority and obedience-based ethics in much of his work. Here he tries to avoid inconsistency by basing ethics not on the authority of the legislator – whose function is to promote conduct that maximizes common ends – but on something more fundamental, on the very *source* of the legislator's ends.

Evidence, logic, argument – all fall flat in the presence of passionate rhetoric. Therefore, at its foundation, Russell believes, ethics depends on the way of the preacher; it is the preacher who leads others to accept new ends and attitudes, who deals with what we wish people to '*feel* in the way of attitudes and desires'. The preacher's method is one of emotional persuasion, an attempt to arouse desired emotions in listeners. It does not involve a primary appeal to evidence, and is little concerned with an appearance of objectivity. Russell writes: 'Every attempt to persuade people that something is good (or bad) in itself, and not merely in its effects, depends upon the art of rousing feelings, not upon an appeal to evidence.'[17] The only criterion for success is the creation of the intended emotion in the preacher's audience, 'similar to his own – or dissimilar if he is a hypocrite'.[18] In matters of morality, Russell believes emotional appeal may be the only *effective* method – that is, it may have some practical justification despite its questionable honesty, as discussed in the previous chapter. And centuries of preaching plus modern research into suggestibility and propaganda indicate that it certainly is effective.

Given the vast potential of this method for abuse and manipulation – the very term 'preacher's method' brings a rush of examples to mind – combining emotional with intellectual appeals may be the most cautious tactic. Aiken notes that we are always, in some way, *persuaded* to adopt all of our convictions and attitudes – by reason, evidence, rhetoric, emotive connotations, faith and so forth. Our convictions do not emerge independently in our mind, nor do we just accept proposed convictions and attitudes because they are presented to us. Something more is needed. So, Aiken concludes: 'It is not rhetoric we object to but its *misuse*: its use as a *substitute* for reason when the latter is available or appropriate.'[19] Reason plays a role – in judging possible consequences, in discovering new objects worthy of desire, and to find the best means to an end.

Even so, 'Questions of evidence or relevance are now wholly subordinated to the practical task of gaining acceptance of the desired proposal.'[20] The preacher has the positive power to transform our desires from personal to universal: 'And preachers may be, in one sense, justified, if they produce the "worthy" end of inciting *moral* attitudes.'[21] Nonetheless, one cannot help but find the preacher's activity worrisome. Whatever the desirability of its results, it is plainly manipulative in its rejection of reason, even if combined with 'facts', just as the most effective lies contain some grain of truth. By Russell's own standards in some of his other writings – his obsession with freedoms of all sorts, for instance – there is something distasteful in encouraging manipulation, no matter what name we give it. There is a difference between persuasion through rhetoric and persuasion through reason. The latter involves an attempt to demonstrate the truth of a claim; the former, as we have discussed, *may* work best by convincing people that an ethical judgment is true, when in fact it is *not even capable* of truth. And can we expect most people to desire themselves acquiescent (or ignorant) victims of such manipulation, even if the end product is a better world? Using Russell's own theory, could we say 'The preacher's method is good'? – that is, 'Would that everyone desired to be manipulated'? I doubt it.[22]

But Russell has a positive opinion of the preacher's method, second only to Stevenson's enthusiastic endorsement. When we are faced with such an utterance as 'you ought to do X', Russell writes, we are really being told that someone else wishes us to desire his end. Usually, it is an authority of some sort. Russell explains:

> If you say to me "you ought to do so-and-so," the motive power of your remark lies in my desire for your approval – together, possibly, with rewards and punishments attached to your approval or disapproval. Since all behaviour springs from desire [and aversion], it is clear that ethical notions can have no importance except as they influence desire. They do this through the desire for approval and the fear of disapproval.[23]

The preacher and propagandist wield enormous power, therefore, especially if we have been taught to regard them as authorities. Without them, without ethical judgments used in this way, perhaps we would not care about universal ends at all. As a psychological egoist, Russell did not believe that we naturally value the ends of others. Without the influence of the preacher and the propagandist, he believes, few of us would care about anything other than our own narrow interests.

The Meaning of 'Good'

The concepts of 'the Good' and 'value' aid, and have aided, in our ongoing liberation from rule-based ethics.[24] When philosophers speak of the Good, *intrinsic* good, Russell claims, they tend to mean 'something we would like to exist for its own sake'. The right follows from the Good: 'Once the Good is defined, the rest of ethics follows. We ought to act in the way we believe most likely to create as much good as possible and as little as possible of its correlative evil.'[25] As soon as we have decided what is good, the right is a matter for science. In philosophically informed systems of ethics, rules are subordinate to their furtherance of intrinsic good. They have no independent value. However, although we can appeal to argument and evidence to settle disagreements over the means to achieve a commonly desired end, such tools are useless, irrelevant, in debates over ends. 'I cannot, therefore, prove that my view of the good life is right; I can only state my view, and hope that as many as possible will agree.'[26] In the end, 'good' remains undefined and perhaps indefinable. When it comes to the Good, 'there is no evidence either way; each disputant can only appeal to his own emotions [and attitudes], and employ such rhetorical devices as shall rouse similar emotions [and attitudes] in others'.[27] Ends stem from desires, desires which change due to circumstances, beliefs, the time and place in which we live, and even minute chemical changes in our bodies.

The *meaning* of 'good' is connected with desire. '*Prima facie*, anything that we all desire is "good" and anything that we all dread is "bad".'[28] We will take this as a loose stipulative definition. The word 'all' is significant, for it indicates that moral judgments have some sort of objectivity and universality – they are an attempt to *escape* from subjectivity. In an ethical dispute, Albert attempts to show Bertha that his desires 'have some quality which makes them more worthy of respect' than hers and they each try to find support by appealing to others who share their desires.[29] To escape from a conflict of desires we can try to 'prove' to our adversary that our desires possess a quality that makes them more worthy of respect. Yet, since no such quality exists, we are not likely to be successful unless our adversary shares other desires with us, to which we may appeal. Alternatively, we could attempt to capitalize on our adversary's insecurities by demonstrating that our desires are shared by most people, or that they are compatible with the desires of most people, while his are not. In other words, we may attempt to universalize our desires. If your desires cannot be harmonized with those of others, society condemns you justly – you are, in essence, working against the interests of the herd. Any of your desires that cannot be harmonized with those of the community are detrimental to that community. Would that no one desired what you desire. We will discover that this sort of claim leads to trouble.

Although he claims otherwise, Russell obviously believes that desires can have a quality that makes them worthy of respect: universalizability. 'Ethics is . . . closely related to politics: it is an attempt to bring back collective desires of a group to bear upon individuals; or . . . it is an attempt by an individual to cause his desires to become those of his group.'[30] To achieve the latter, his desires must be in harmony 'with the general interest' or general desires; thus self-interest and societal interest must, in at least some respects, be capable of *mutual* satisfaction. When we succeed at this game, self-deception, always a powerful force in ethics and politics, steps in: we come to believe we have discovered objective, universal, value. It is Russell's hope that recognition of ethical subjectivity, in the sense that there are no moral 'facts' to be discovered, might counterbalance our self-deceptions.[31]

Russell owes a debt to Kant in his contention that, if we cannot universalize a 'principle of action', it is not moral.[32] To say a desire can be universalized is to say that it does not conflict with the general desires of most human beings, it is in harmony with them, it can be realized alongside them – it is 'mature'. Any desire that cannot be universalized, that undermines the general desires of the human race, the desires common to most human beings, *cannot* be moral. So morality is objective and universal concerning its subject matter: the collective and general desires of humanity. This is how ethics relates to politics, and explains why Russell said ethics 'has a certain kind of political objectivity' – an *interpersonal objectivity*.

But what of the desire to have someone to hate? Human beings seem to derive scads of enjoyment from having an object of derision, loathing, or abuse. One could argue that this is one of the most common of human desires. How could Russell make sense of it? The problem is not as serious as it first appears, for this very desire is incompossible with other general desires because the actions to which it leads (perhaps necessarily) interfere with a host of other desires – such as desires for comfort, security, and peace. Because of these conflicts, we are forced to decide between the desire for someone to hate and, say, the desire for peace. The latter is universalizable, compossible to a greater degree, and stems from Russell's criteria, of which we will soon have more to say. That the former desire is common makes no difference.

Only those desires and attitudes governed by general interest or sympathy can be called moral. In Russell's opinion, the purpose of ethics is to help us learn to extend our sympathies and take into account desires other than our own – in other words, to widen the scope of our desires to include the other members of society. We cannot reasonably expect others to accept moral rules which are not in accordance with humanity's common desires. We *can* reasonably expect others to adopt our moral judgments if they express desires common to all, or most, people – even if the list of such desires is short. So if a moral judgment expressed only an *individual's* desires, it would *not* be moral. As Aiken aptly restates it, 'Thus the main function of moral judgments and of ethics is to depersonalize our desires; it is only then that we are moral beings.'[33]

But why should we care about the general desires of humanity? Would not Russell be forced to admit that we will not care unless we already have a desire to benefit our fellow human beings? Russell believes that we have no reason to privilege one person's desires over another's; the desires of all are equal, at least in the eyes of the legislator. Fine, but that gives us no reason to care about anyone else's desires. And Russell believes that, naturally, we don't care about anyone else's desires. The answer, of course, appeals to self-interest. We should care about the desires of others, we should take them into account, because in the end we will benefit.

At times, by 'maturity' Russell seems to mean 'enlightened self-interest'.

Sure – yet some of us could benefit even more by taking advantage of those who follow the rules. Russell is not alone in facing this problem, for it has plagued moral philosophy for a very long time. Be that as it may, and although he fares no worse than his predecessors or successors, his solution is unconvincing. He hopes that we will gradually reduce the likelihood of abusers through increasingly effective moral education.

Love and Knowledge

We move now to Russell's conception of ethical sentences, a conception in most respects similar to those of Ayer and Stevenson. Sentences concerning intrinsic value, such as 'Happiness is intrinsically good', have the same grammatical form as the sentence, 'X is square'. But, Russell insists, the two are not *logically* similar, for ethical sentences do not actually state anything. They are only statements in a secondary sense – inasmuch and insofar as they affirm our personal desires, interpreted as 'I wish everybody to desire happiness'. In this sense, ethical sentences are matters of psychology, since they assert psychological facts about the speaker. But the *primary* meaning of such sentences is *emotive*, affirming a universal desire: 'Would that everyone desired this!'[34] In its primary sense, an ethical sentence 'states nothing but desires something' – and since it states nothing it cannot be true or false.[35] Despite that fact, *an ethical sentence is objective in content, direction, and object.* As Aiken interprets him, correctly I should think, 'When I say "X is good" I am expressing my own wish that everyone desire X. But the *object* of my wish is universal and hence objective. . . . the desires and interests of humanity.'[36] The natural response to all of this is 'Sure, *sometimes*' – but we must remember that Russell is offering a *stipulative* definition; he is defining ethics proper, as he understands it, and is little concerned at this point with what others may understand ethics to be.[37]

Thus Russell could be called a 'universalistic emotivist'.[38] Ethical sentences are expressions of personal desires that are impersonal in that they have a universal object: the collective general desires of humanity. To make his point clear, Russell contrasts the following sentences: (a) 'All Chinese are Buddhists' – a statement of fact, refutable, capable of truth or falsity; (b) 'I believe that all Chinese are Buddhists' – a statement of belief only refutable by showing that the speaker does not really believe what he says he believes, and which makes an assertion regarding a private state of mind; and (c) 'Beauty is Good' – which means both 'Would that everyone loved the beautiful' (primary meaning) or 'I wish that everybody loved the beautiful' (secondary meaning). The first meaning is not a statement and makes no assertion. It is an optative expression of a wish; 'Beauty is Good' is merely similar in superficial *form* to (a) in that it seems to be a declarative statement of objective, or external, fact. It belongs to the realm of ethics. The second meaning does make an assertion but only about the speaker's state of mind – just like (b). It is a matter of psychology. The optative meaning is that which is specific to ethics, and in that sense ethics does not contain statements that are true or false, just universalizable desires.

That one's wish for everyone to adopt a certain desire is personal and subjective – even though *what* one desires is universal, impersonal and objective – is the key difference between Russell's later emotivism and the theories of Ayer and Stevenson. The latter two believed that much of the confusion in ethics was caused by the similarity of form between ethical and factual sentences. Russell might agree, but he also believes that 'It is . . .

this curious *interlocking of the particular and the universal* which has caused so much confusion in ethics.'[39] And Russell, to be sure, has his own opinion as to what ought to be valued. In a famous statement, he writes, '*The good life is one inspired by love and guided by knowledge.*'[40] In this context, 'knowledge', of course, refers to knowledge in the only sense Russell finds meaningful: 'scientific' knowledge, knowledge of facts. Such knowledge is not irrelevant to our desires, for we may use it to help us discover the most effective means of achieving our desired ends. He believes there is remarkable agreement when it comes to what is good. Most ethical controversy arises as to the best *means* for achieving the Good, and disputes of that sort can be settled by reason, argument and evidence. These controversies are scientific, not moral, matters.

On what basis can Russell, as an emotivist, make any claims about which things are good? First, he may say that *knowledge and love* are what he desires everyone to desire – 'Would that everyone desired knowledge and love'. On another level, he desires everyone to desire a life 'inspired by love and guided by knowledge' – 'Would that everyone desired a life inspired by love and guided by knowledge'. Are these desires simply arbitrary products of Russell's preferences, which in turn are products of his upbringing, circumstances, and so forth? In some sense, yes. But he surely believes that these particular ends are either common to all or most people, or that, were people aware of the consequences of desiring love and knowledge (and a life inspired by them), they would desire them. These goods are universalizable and maximally compossible. They do not lead people into conflict, and they make possible the satisfaction of many other desires.

Defences and Explanations

Pigden writes: 'Not only did Russell anticipate Ayer and Stevenson – his version of emotivism is distinctly superior to the versions they went on to invent.'[41] He is correct. We have already examined Ayer's and Stevenson's versions of emotivism, finding both (along with Russell's early attempt) wanting. Now we will discover why Russell's later version is superior, and discuss the challenges it still faces.

The theories of Ayer and Stevenson are often unjustly criticized for being incapable of dealing with moral contradictions, because they insist that moral judgments merely express feelings or attitudes of approval and disapproval. Russell's mature theory avoids these criticisms from the outset.[42] In his enlightened emotivism, two wishful expressions – for example, 'Would that everyone desired pleasure!' and 'Would that no one desired pleasure!' – can be contradictory because both cannot possibly be realized. They are *incompossible.* Just as logic requires a notion of incompatibility for propositions, so emotivism requires a corresponding notion for desire. The logical relation between two desires, and thus between ethical claims, is one of compossibility. Two *desires* are incompatible if they cannot be jointly realized, compatible if they can be. Thus, the *sentences* expressing those desires – 'X is good' and 'X is bad' – can contradict one another.

Although we found that Stevenson's theory, at least, could benefit from a similar defence, that possibility was not immediately apparent. Once Russell's theory is understood, it is far more difficult to raise the objection in the first place.

On a related note, another crucial advantage is that 'Russell's theory allows for logical relations between moral judgments. . . . We can define a consequence relation for optatives such that optative B is a consequence of the set of optatives A and a (possibly empty) set of propositions C, if A cannot be realized under circumstances C unless B is realized too.'[43] Thus, 'an optative argument is valid if the conclusion is an optative consequence of the premises, invalid otherwise'.[44] To explain: if I say 'Happiness is good', I am expressing a desire for everyone to desire happiness. Let us say that in the present circumstances, this desire cannot be realized unless another desire, expressed by 'Pleasure is good', can also be realized. That is, it is impossible, given the circumstances, for the desire for happiness to be realized unless we also desire pleasure. In this case, therefore, the desire for pleasure is an optative consequence of the desire for happiness *and* the given circumstances. Stevenson, on the other hand, will not bend from the position that validity is a matter of *truth*, with the result that ethical judgments have no place in semantically valid arguments. Since we distinguish between valid and invalid ethical arguments, and since Russell's theory can account for this practice, Russell's theory is superior in this respect to both Stevenson's and Ayer's.

Russell's enlightened emotivism also avoids the trap of vicious circularity that claims the others.[45] We saw Ayer and Stevenson fail as a consequence of defining 'good' and 'bad' as approval and disapproval. On the other hand, Russell now claims that 'X is good' expresses a *desire*, a desire for everyone to desire X. This one small difference allows him to escape the circularity of his successors.[46]

Ayer's theory depends on the verification principle. To what degree Russell agrees or disagrees with the reasoning behind the verification principle makes no practical difference, for his theory is not in any way dependent upon it. If anything, it depends primarily on his views of the nature of desire (and impulse, as we will discover) in relation to moral judgment.

A common, and facile, objection to Russell's emotivism charges that it leads to immorality and irrationality – a claim that obviously assumes a very different conception of 'immoral' to that used by Russell.[47] Yet because he takes it seriously, and because his defence sheds some more light on his theory, it is worth considering.

First, these critics claim, did Russell not indicate that a recognition of emotivism would lead us to reject the concepts of sin and vindictive punishment?[48] They are, in Russell's opinion confused about the facts, for the practical consequences of his theory are better than those of absolutist theories – they can hardly be worse. The concepts of sin and vindictive punishment, which stem from absolutist ethics, have caused immeasurable suffering to no discernible benefit, and they are not universalizable, so they ought to be discarded. Their rejection is positive from the perspectives of Russell's emotivism and his rule-consequentialism.

What about moral obligation? Russell does not believe that his theory logically entails the abandonment of moral obligation and responsibility, and he is correct. 'Moral obligation, if it is to influence conduct, must consist not merely of a belief [regarding the consequences of our actions] but of a desire'.[49] A desire for the approval of others; at bottom, a desire to bring about generally desired consequences. Moral obligation does not involve an abstract duty to promote the Good. It is an obligation to satisfy the general desires of humanity that *has no power* over anyone who does not share those desires.[50] Although this feature may lead some to conclude that Russell's theory has no imperative power, his point is that the more common conception of duty, based on a belief in 'objective' good, has no such power either. The belief in the 'objectivity' of ethics is irrelevant in this case. 'The sort of life that most of us admire is one which is guided by large impersonal desires; now such desires can, no doubt, be encouraged by example, education and knowledge, but they can hardly be created by the mere abstract belief that they are good, nor discouraged by an analysis of what is meant by the word "good".'[51] Russell's theory lauds lives guided by universal, impersonal desires, desires for the realization of everyone's desires. It extols benevolence, compassion, sympathy. In what way could such a theory lead to immorality? Indeed, what does 'immorality' mean in this objection? In Aiken's words:

> Our impersonal desires, which are created as we recognize the desires of mankind, produce their own morality. Without these general desires no matter what our ethical theory may be, our conduct cannot be moral and will not serve mankind. Hence no matter how we may define value, no matter what our theoretical ethics may be, our strength as moral beings lies in the presence of impersonal desires in our souls.[52]

In *Power*, Russell indulges in greater detail. He writes: 'The great ethical innovators have not been men who *knew* more than others, they have been men who *desired* more, or, to be more accurate, men whose desires were more impersonal and of larger scope than those of average men.'[53] They desired everyone's happiness, and when they discovered that most did not share their desire, they wished otherwise – hence, 'Happiness is good', i.e., 'Would that everyone desired happiness!'. The universality of their desires grew out of limitless sympathy, whereas most of us are rather stingy when it comes to sympathy. We may extend it to some – say family, friends, social class, nation, ethnicity – but not all. True universal sympathy 'is the analogue, in the realm of feeling, of impersonal curiosity in the realm of intellect; both alike are essential elements in mental growth'.[54]

Russell, like Hume, believes ethics is practical – he recognizes an aspect of the essential purpose of moral theories that Ayer and Stevenson did not. Moral theories ought to explain, and make possible, moral judgments. And the purpose of making a moral judgment is to lead us to moral action. Further, we are not merely motivated by desire, but by beliefs and emotion as well. We must *care* about the end if we are to act for it. Thus, an adequate account of moral obligation requires a role for desire and emotion as well as belief[55] – perhaps more so. No amount of moral teaching and exhortation will influence our conduct unless we desire the good, Aiken writes, 'unless in fact we possess *desires* which are impersonal'.[56] Thus, benevolence and sympathy – the very models of impersonal desires, if you will – are the 'essential stimuli' to a moral life. In what appears to be a contradiction of strict psychological egoism, Russell writes:

> Our desires are, in fact, more general and less purely selfish than many moralists imagine; if it were not so, no theory of ethics would make moral improvement possible. It is, in fact, not by ethical theory but by the cultivation of large and generous desires through intelligence, happiness, and freedom from fear, that men can be brought to act more than they do at present in a manner that is consistent with the general happiness of mankind.[57]

The point is that you have to *desire* this happiness. Whether we wish to recognize it or not, our only rational recourse in a moral dispute is to attempt to influence another's desires, and through them, her conduct. Theory, evidence and argument can be used to change our beliefs, which influence our desires to some extent, but desire has the most important role.

If one lacks such grand impersonal desires, one's conduct will only be socially useful if one's interests are in harmony with those of society. Thus, we need to create such harmony to the greatest possible extent. 'When you meet a man with whom you have a fundamental ethical disagreement . . . you will find yourself no better able to cope with him if you believe in objective values than if you do not.'[58] It is not true that, 'if a general desire, say for the happiness of mankind, has not the sanction of absolute good, it is in some way irrational. This is due to a lingering belief in objective values'.[59] Rationality and irrationality do not apply to desires. Reason's task 'is to show us how to realize our desires'.[60] Reason can show us the means.

That Russell's theory lacks an 'element of command' along the lines of Kant's categorical imperative is obvious. His critics believe this is a defect, though they may be unable to articulate why. 'Ethics is a social force which helps a society to cohere,' Russell writes, 'and every one who utters an ethical judgment feels himself in some sense a legislator or a judge, according to the degree of generality of the judgment in question.'[61] The questionable assumption, made by Russell's critics, is that moral judgments have some sort of force if they are as objective as judgments of fact. Russell sympathizes – he often feels the same way. Nonetheless, he finds no truth in this conviction. A judgment of fact is either true or false, our opinions in the matter notwithstanding. Moral judgments, like it or not, are simply incapable of truth or falsity. No matter what one might prefer, 'Would that everyone desired pudding!' (assuming this relates to a general collective desire for pudding) will never be true.

Still, we seek some sort of persuasive force in our ethical theories. We take it for granted that a fully adequate moral theory will have some sort of persuasive power, an element of command – that is part of its applicability. The fact that all or most 'objective' theories lack such an element may be a reason to reject them, but it does not excuse Russell from a responsibility to provide it. When one is creating a theory of ethics, one should try to make that theory as persuasive as possible – even if that requires addressing assumptions that seem baseless. Whether moral judgments have a truth-value or not, we expect an element of command in any adequate moral theory. Russell has not proven that our expectation is misguided. On the other hand, because his contention that 'objectivity' gives us no more force than 'subjectivity' is correct, his theory's lack of force makes it no worse than any other. Furthermore, his metaethic is tied to his consequentialism, so he may use any element of command that consequentialism can provide.

Russell does not believe the difference between factual judgments and moral judgments is all that important. He uses the example of persuasion to illustrate why. In matters of fact or science, an appeal to evidence is highly persuasive.[62] Controversies, therefore, do not last long – unless politics, religion and other emotional forces obfuscate the facts involved, as they have done in the needless controversy over evolution. In these cases, 'Such questions are normally decided by rhetoric, brass bands, and broken heads.'[63] Regardless, 'the detached scientist, if he exists, may, neglected and alone, persist in applying scientific methods even to questions that rouse passion'.[64] Note that in such matters, a moral belief and/or judgment is involved. As Russell writes: 'In the matter of persuasion it is often overlooked that the advocate of scientific methods must – since persuading is a practical activity – base himself on the ethical principle that it is better to believe truth than falsehood.'[65] In the language of Russell's emotivism, the scientist wishes everyone believed truly, and that everyone believed as he does. Values – universalizable desires – are involved even in the superficially 'objective' work of science.

In moral, political and religious disputes – that is, in controversies *about* values – persuasion is a different matter. Propagandists 'wish people to have different beliefs, which they may themselves entertain, but which they seldom wish to see subjected to a scientific scrutiny'.[66] In a moral dispute, one attempts to inspire in the other emotion one feels in oneself. This is what preaching is all about, 'and it was my purpose in the various books in which I have expressed ethical opinions. The art of presenting one's desires persuasively is totally different from that of logical demonstration, but it is equally legitimate.'[67]

As do Ayer and Stevenson, Russell does not believe there can be any rational debate once we reach the level of ends. To require a moral theory to account for such debate may be illegitimate. In Aiken's words: 'In one sense, then, there is no rational justification for our basic approvals, just because they are basic. They are not justified; they are used to justify. They are neither true nor false. They just are.'[68] An interesting possibility. Russell may have had such an argument in mind, though I expect he would have been uncomfortable with it, given that his entire career was, in part, inspired by his discomfort with the axioms of Euclidean geometry.[69]

Perhaps the greatest advantage of Russell's refined emotivism for one with his tendencies is that it allows one 'to moralize with a clean intellectual conscience'.[70] That a moral theory must at least make moral decision-making possible is a requirement of his theory. But *how* can an emotivist moralize consistently? He explained how in his 'Reply to Criticisms', published in *The Philosophy of Bertrand Russell* (1944), a remarkable paper in which Russell, in Pigden's words, 'reaffirms his belief in the emotivism of *Religion and Science*, and urges that emotivism is not inconsistent with moral vehemence or moral commitment. The moral vocabulary provides us with the verbal machinery to express certain preferences. Since he has the relevant preferences, he is surely entitled to use this machinery to express them.'[71]

Russell dealt explicitly with the apparent incompatibility between his metaethic and his moral crusades, the charge that he was inconsistent at best, hypocritical at worst – just as he had during the First World War. Yes, he admits, 'although I hold ethical valuations to be subjective, I nevertheless allow myself emphatic opinions on ethical questions'.[72] Perhaps he could avoid the charge by refusing to speak out on matters of moral import, but such a strategy would make him insincere. Besides, 'an inconsistent system may well contain less falsehood than a consistent one'.[73] One may, after all, be consistently false.

Though he is a philosopher, he remains a human being, one who is 'not prepared to forgo my right to feel and express ethical passions; no amount of logic, even though it be my own, will persuade me that I ought to do so'.[74] Russell has likes and dislikes, abhorrences and admirations, as does every other human being. Whether his moral feelings are grounded in factual propositions or not is beside the point. 'Pleasure in the spectacle of cruelty horrifies me', he writes, 'and I am not ashamed of the fact that it does. I am no more prepared to give up all this than I am to give up the multiplication table.'[75] Although he does not believe he is inconsistent in this regard, it does not matter. He would not stop venting his 'ethical passions' even if he were.

Nonetheless, like Ayer, he argues that in most cases, moral disagreements over an act, which 'can usually, though not always, be reduced to a difference as to means', are matters for science to handle. He clarifies the point quite nicely in the following passage:

Let us consider two theories as to the good. One says, like Christianity, Kant, and democracy: whatever the good may be, any one man's enjoyment of it has the same value as any other man's. The other says: there is a certain sub-class of mankind – white men, Germans, gentiles, or what not – whose good and evil alone counts in an estimation of ends; other men are only to be considered as means. I shall suppose that A takes the first view, and B the second. What can either say to convince the other of error? I can only imagine arguments that would be strictly irrelevant. A might say: If you ignore the interests of a large part of mankind, they will rebel and murder you. B might say: The portion of mankind that I favour is so much superior to the rest in skill and courage that it is sure to rule in any case, so why not frankly acknowledge the true state of affairs? Each of these is an argument as to means, not as to ends. When such arguments are swept away, there remains, so far as I can see, nothing to be said except for each party to express moral disapproval of the other. Those who reject this conclusion advance no argument against it except that it is unpleasant.[76]

Though we have seen that Russell recognizes the role of beliefs as an indirect cause of desire, he does not appear to go far enough. This may be the only issue on which Ayer and Stevenson are superior. For instance, in the above example, he appears to ignore the possibility of convincing the other party by debating the reasons *behind* that party's beliefs. What are they based upon? Does not the privileging of one party's desires over another's require some sort of justification?[77] If we can convince our adversary that his beliefs are false, that his reasoning is faulty, or that he has not understood the implications of his convictions, we may indirectly change his desires – thus, his ends. Yes, Russell appears to acknowledge this possibility at times, and it is consistent with his theory, but he does not appear to appreciate its full significance. Although attitudes and desire may not be capable of rational justification or falsification, the beliefs that encourage them and make them seem attractive *are*.

The principal point against his critics is that *there is no inconsistency* in an emotivist expressing moral outrage or embarking on campaigns of activism. Russell expressed surprise that people assumed inconsistency in his outspoken moral opinions, for: 'By my own theory I am, in doing so, expressing vehement desires as to the desires of mankind. I feel such desires, so why not express them?'[78] His moralism is quite in line with the thesis of emotivism itself. As Pigden writes, 'The moralising emotivist . . . is an honest man who uses moral language for its express purpose.'[79] Moral outrage uses moral vocabulary to express desires. The expression of moral judgments does not in itself imply that they have a truth-value.

Russell's opponents appear to believe that emotivism forbids moral outrage because it removes the possibility of *justification* for that outrage. Indeed it may, but why would outrage – the expression of moral disapproval – need justification at all? And if it did, what could possibly justify it? Perhaps Russell could turn to his consequentialism to justify these expressions, if he really felt the need. He could say, for instance, that moral outrage is justified if it furthers the realization of universal desires. And all he needs to mean by 'justified', in this instance, is that moral outrage is an effective means to his end. Nevertheless, since we have no prima facie reason to believe that moral outrage requires justification, nor that anyone is obliged to pay attention to someone else's outrage, I find the objection most unconvincing.

Unlike Ayer and Stevenson, Russell provides a basis for moral criticism – side-stepping Toulmin's criticisms. As Aiken states:

> for Russell particular desires can be moral or immoral. When we *morally* disapprove of someone, we are criticizing his desires and actions from the standpoint of a disinterested observer. Russell believed that there is a criterion by which we are enabled to judge which desires are to be approved as "moral", i.e. those desires which are guided by love and knowledge. This criterion determines what we understand as a "moral desire". No one can be logically forced to accept it.[80]

Yet, what if I have no desire to live a life inspired by love and guided by knowledge? Am I under some sort of obligation to have this desire? If I do not have it, am I obliged to act as though I do? Russell does not appear to believe that we are under any obligation to live a 'moral' life, nor are we under an obligation to feel any 'moral' desires. However, if we want to get along with others in a civil society, we at least ought to act *as though* we have such desires. On this point, Russell is no stronger or weaker than any other moral philosopher. No moral theory can force us to be moral or to have moral desires – how could it? Objective or subjective, absolutist or relativist, we cannot be *forced* to feel or act morally.

Whereas the emotivisms of Ayer and Stevenson provided no basis for choosing between two available courses of action, Russell's clearly does, though it may not be entirely effective. We are to act on the basis of universalizable, impersonal, desires. But might we find ourselves in a situation in which two courses of action are both compossible with the general desires of humanity? In that situation, which should we choose? It wouldn't matter. Recall Toulmin's example of two people being told to choose different courses of action. Although Russell could say that the two were contradicting each other, he could not provide a basis for choosing one over the other if both were inspired by a universalizable and maximally compossible desire. It is not clear why he would need to, anyway. Perhaps either course of action would be acceptable.

We find that Russell's enlightened emotivism also escapes another of Toulmin's criticisms: that emotivism incorrectly assumes that the test of accuracy for moral terms is necessarily self-referential, just because it is sometimes so. Were that the case, Toulmin argued, a complete answer to 'Is this good?' would be impossible. Russell's peculiar marriage of subjectivity and objectivity keeps him from falling prey. The answer to 'Is this good?' is 'Yes, if it is compatible with the general collective desires of humanity.' His theory can also account for the difference between moral and non-moral values – the first concern universalizable and maximally compossible desires; the second do not. And this is a standard which we can conceive of everyone agreeing upon (however unlikely!). Whether people in fact agree upon such a standard is irrelevant – if everyone agreed on a standard, we would not be discussing the issue. Russell is not concerned with what standard everyone does in fact accept, but with a standard that everyone *could* accept.[81]

When it comes to whether the *strength* of a desire is relevant to ethical decision-making, Russell is silent. For example, does a powerful desire matter more than a weak desire? Is an overwhelming desire for immense wealth worth more than a half-hearted desire for child welfare? Although he does not address the issue directly, his possible response is clear. All that matters is the universalizability of one's desires. Deciding whether this is so includes a consideration of a desire's compossibility with one's other universalizable desires, and those of others. So we must ask: can a desire for immense wealth be universal? Is it capable of joint satisfaction with universal desires – such as those for security, freedom and comfort? Perhaps, perhaps not in the present world. But a desire for child welfare clearly makes the cut.

Furthermore, we must keep in mind Russell's criteria for moral criticism. Is a desire for immense wealth inspired by love and guided by knowledge? There is some knowledge involved, obviously. For instance, my desire for immense wealth may be guided by the knowledge that it would lead to greater personal comfort. But is it inspired by love, which we may take as compassion and sympathy for others? Again, probably not. That money must come from somewhere. We could argue that one could desire wealth so that it could be used to look after the destitute. In that case, the desire for immense wealth would be a means to the satisfaction of a universalizable desire, and we could argue that both are inspired by love and guided by knowledge. Russell does not mention desires as means for the achievement of universally desired ends, though it seems to be unavoidable.

Pigden mentions some objections that Russell cannot dodge. His weakest is that Russell 'provides no good reason to believe' his theory.[82] Russell certainly believed he had. His reasoning was, to restate it in stronger terms, that we have had millennia to come up with a satisfactory argument to prove the existence of intrinsic value, and we have failed. Although this, in itself, does not prove that there is no such thing, it is a strong prima facie reason to try a new approach. Additionally, Russell could think of no compelling reason to assume the existence of intrinsic values, and since he believed we could explain ethics without them, Occam's razor demands they be cut. Were that not enough, and Russell appeared to believe it was, he thought there might be a pragmatic-consequentialist reason to believe his theory: it could lead to great benefit. So he felt justified both by the inability of 'objective' and absolutist theories to establish the external existence of values, by the apparent superfluity of such values and by the expected practical consequences of his theory.

The more serious objection, relayed by Pigden, comes from P.T. Geach.[83] Consider: P1 – 'It is good as an end that people cultivate the arts.' P2 – 'If it is good as an end that people cultivate the arts, then it is good as a means that they should have the funding to do so.' And C – 'Therefore: It is good as a means that people should have the funding to cultivate the arts.' What does 'It is good as an end that people cultivate the arts' mean in P2? In P1 it is an assertion, and Russell's theory can make sense of it. But one could assent to P2 without any sort of desire for P1; that is, one could assent to P2 without desiring that people desire the cultivation of the arts, since it is merely a hypothetical statement. Such contexts are not uncommon – they may, in fact, be nearly inescapable – so Pigden concludes that Russell's theory is incomplete.

Geach and Pigden have a good point and, as Pigden notes, the remaining modern emotivists struggle with this same problem to no satisfactory resolution. Yet, perhaps Geach and Pigden are confusing two different uses of the word 'good'. One could understand P2 as a statement about effective means to an end desired by some who wish that everyone shared their universalizable and maximally-compossible desire. The speaker needn't share the desire to make the statement.

One of the most interesting aspects of Russell's theory is its use of personal and interpersonal compossibility. However, it leads to some possible criticisms. Personally, compossibility is a matter of egoism. It is in one's best interests to have compossible desires. But what can Russell say about desires that are incompossible with those of others, but compossible with one's other desires? Take stealing, for example. It may be the case that a desire to steal someone else's property does not conflict with any of my other desires, though it conflicts with the rightful owner's desire to possess her property and feel secure. What course of action should I take in this case? Whose desires should take precedence?

At first, Russell does not appear to have any theoretical basis for ranking interpersonal compossibility above self-compossibility, though he seems to assume it. But, again, perhaps we are ignoring Russell's criteria of moral criticism. My desire to steal someone else's property is not compossible with desires for universal love and knowledge. I love myself over others if I prioritize my needs over theirs. In fact, any desire that is incompossible with the general desires of humanity – that is, the universalizable desires – is immoral according to Russell's theory. So it is not really a question of my desires versus the desires of others after all, since my universalizable desires are included among the general desires of humanity. There is a theoretical basis, but it is not immediately obvious.

Might Russell's criteria lead us into a Robin Hood scenario, however? It appears to allow us to steal from the rich to give to the poor. Such behaviour could be motivated by love and compassion, guided by knowledge that our actions are likely to help a great many people, that a certain amount of money would allow them to buy a certain amount of food, and so forth. Much appears to depend on how we *characterize* the operative desire and corresponding moral judgment. We might say we're motivated by a desire for greater happiness in the world – stealing small amounts of money from a lot of people to feed a sizeable number who would not otherwise be fed. Surely their happiness will be greater than the irritation of a billionaire who's been robbed of $10 (or even $100). The expression used may be: 'Would that everyone desired to feed the poor and hungry'. Is the theft motivated by this expressed desire, or a desire to steal from the rich? We could not expect the latter to be universaliz-able – the rich, at the very least, would not accept it. But if this desire is what motivates the behaviour, Russell's criteria would condemn the activity. Nothing about the activity itself has changed, only the character – or perhaps merely the *description* – of its motivational desire. We will return to this problem in the next chapter, where it becomes more complicated.

For now, let us turn to another potential problem generated by the application of Russell's theory. Suppose we have two men, Albert and Barney, who desire to have a homosexual relation-ship. This relationship is incompossible with the desires of two million Christian fundamentalists who disapprove, who exclaim, 'Would that no one desired homosexual relationships'. In fact, the majority of people in the world today probably disapprove of homosexuality, so we could say, with confidence, that it is incompossible with the desires of most people.[84] Does this mean that a desire for a homosexual-free world is *good* – and that the desire of the two homosexuals is *bad*? One might even say, in the case of the fundamentalists, that their desire is motivated by universalizable desires for love and knowledge, thus meeting Russell's criteria. For, if they buy St. Paul's claims, their love for all people may lead them to condemn homosexuality in the hope of saving the souls of homosexuals – a love guided by their knowledge of Paul's condemnation, regardless of whether Paul himself had any knowledge regarding salvation.

I expect that the problem here, as earlier, is one of deciding which desires are motivating the involved parties. The goodness or badness of a desire depends on how it is characterized, how it is phrased – evaluation, in other words, is description-relative.

But Russell may be able to avoid the problem by generalizing the desire of the fundamentalists into a class, then demonstrating the consequences of approving of, or desiring, the entire class. For example, in this case, Russell could generalize the desire of the fundamentalists as a desire for others to follow Biblical commands. But this leads to conflict, since many Biblical commands plainly contradict each other. They are incompossible with one another. And the operative desire is incompossible with the desires of many others – we could include similar desires using the Scriptures of Islam, Buddhism, etc. in this class by generalizing it further. Even if we did not take that route, the desire in question is incompossible with the desire of some atheists for people to ignore the Bible entirely.

It is a weak defence. The fundamentalists in question could use the age-old strategy of claiming to hate the sin and love the sinner, for example. And they might mean it sincerely – they may actually love the sinner no matter how much they despise the sin. In this case, they could say that their desire was inspired by love.

On the other hand, the desire of our two homosexuals could be generalized as a desire for the freedom of two people in love to enter into a private relationship. Such a desire is more likely to meet Russell's criteria, and less likely to lead to conflict. The crucial component is the level of generality specified. And Russell is not very helpful in this regard. He seems to have quite general desires in mind, but gives no criteria for determining which level of generality, specifically, is to be used in describing the expressed desires. 'Would that no one desired homosexual relationships' may be fairly universalizable, since most people worldwide are at the very least uncomfortable with homosexuality. Knowing this, we can generalize the desire further, as 'Would that no one desired sexual relationships of which I disapprove, or which make me uncomfortable'. At this level, we run into problems, for once the consequences of universalizing this desire were pointed out – many people are uncomfortable about the idea of sexual relations between their parents, after all – few would accept it. What then? Do we accept that this desire, at this level of generality, is not universalizable, but that the previous, less general desire, *is*? Can Russell's criteria be used to show that *the same desire both is and is not universalizable* – depending on its level of generality? Or can one and the same desire be both universalizable and not universalizable, depending only on how it is *described*? If so, Russell's criteria cannot be adequate.

The only route left to us at this point is to examine the knowledge-claims (beliefs) accompanying, and supposedly guiding, each desire. By analyzing the beliefs, linked causally to desires, we may be able to decide which is better 'supported' (to use the word loosely), or perhaps change the desires of one party by exposing the inadequacy of their beliefs. If we were to show some people that their desires were accompanied, perhaps psychologically reinforced, by erroneous beliefs, their beliefs might change. Others would not be affected at all.

By now it should be apparent that, whatever its faults, Russell's enlightened emotivism is superior to the versions created by Ayer and Stevenson. It is also superior to his proto-emotivism of the First World War, in large part because now he actually bothers to set forth a theory – one that attempts to explain a broad range of moral phenomena, provides a basis for moral criticisms and moral decision-making, and manages to rise above subjectivism's foibles by injecting some objectivity into emotivism. Furthermore, Russell's theory may justify itself. If he truly believed that widespread belief in emotivism would lead to great benefit, he could justify advocating it on pragmatic grounds, even if he did not believe emotivism was true. And he could, in fact, defend the advocacy of emotivism while consistently asserting it, just as he does with his moral outrage in the 'Reply to Criticisms'. All he needs to say is 'Would that everyone desired the benefit of all'. If everyone believed in emotivism, society as a whole would benefit. Therefore, it makes good pragmatic sense to advocate emotivism, to try to convince the world that it is the most accurate ethical theory available.

Russell's mixture of ethical subjectivity and objectivity may strike some as odd. It *is* odd, although his peculiar conception of moral intersubjectivity may be one of his theory's greatest strengths as well. It offers us a way out of our limited personal perspectives, a way to understand the difference between moral and non-moral judgments, and gives 'causes' for moral attitudes – all through the recognition of impersonal desires for universal objects. Aiken agrees: 'This is why moral judgments may be significant independently of how the judge himself happens to feel. It is also why moral judgments do not vary in significance in accordance with the variable personal attitudes which may accompany them.'[85]

The other great strength of Russell's enlightened emotivism is its clever use of desire. Although he had made reference to desire in connection with ethics for many years, during this period he made great use of insights developed in *The Analysis of Mind* and *Principles of Social Reconstruction*, both of which appear to have been sadly neglected by those few who study Russell's moral philosophy – and by Russell himself. That is, Russell does not appear to make conscious use of his work on desire and impulse in any of his work on ethics during the enlightened emotivist period, though much of the time he appears to assume its relevance and veracity. In fact, Russell makes no direct reference to that work, most of it done during one of the most tumultuous periods of his life, until he replies to a criticism made by Justus Buchler in 1944. There, in his 'Reply to Criticisms', he implies that a complete understanding of his emotivism must take his work on desire and impulse into account.[86] And perhaps, by taking a closer look at his theories of impulse and desire, and their connection to self-interest, we will come to appreciate the force of his emotivism – its answer to 'Why should I care that you say X is good if it can't be true?'

We will hold off on a full comparison of Russell's enlightened emotivism with the other varieties of emotivism considered in Chapter 2 until we have tried to combine it with his theories of impulse and desire.

Notes

1. Russell's enlightened emotivism was set forth and/or implied in *What I Believe, An Outline of Philosophy, Power,* and, primarily, *Religion and Science.*
2. Russell later reviewed *Language, Truth and Logic* (see Russell, 'Review of A.J. Ayer, Language, Truth, and Logic [1947]', *The Collected Papers of Bertrand Russell, Volume 11,* ed. John G. Slater, (London: Routledge, 1997), 171–3) but did not mention Ayer's emotivism at the time. In a later review of *Philosophical Essays,* Russell treated Ayer's defence of emotivism quite favourably (Russell, 'Light Versus Heat [1954]', ibid., 173–5).
3. Pigden, *RoE,* 131.
4. Russell, *RS,* 175–6.
5. Ibid, 243.
6. Pigden, *RoE,* 132.
7. Bertrand Russell, *An Outline of Philosophy,* Revised edition (London: Routledge, 1995), 184; henceforth 'Russell, OP'. Apparently, most of us have not matured emotionally and intellectually.
8. Hopefully avoiding criticisms from Ross!
9. Ibid., 185.
10. Ibid., 186.
11. Ibid.
12. Aiken, *BRPM,* 106. Russell appears to assume that this is true by definition, that the code of ethics developed by an impartial legislator is one which embodies impersonal moral rules. It is stipulative, and shaky. But since it is reasonable to assume that impersonal rules would follow from the legislator's impartiality, we will allow Russell some leeway in the matter.
13. Whether this would lead to the oppression of minority groups is another issue, best left to a discussion of Russell's rule-consequentialism. I expect Russell believes his theory would prevent the frustration of a minority's *universalizable* desires, and that he would

not care if it frustrated the others. Yet, there appears to be no reason to assume that this would indeed be the case.

14. Russell, *RS*, 234.
15. Ibid.
16. And the community, to its shame, lay behind Russell's dismissal from City College, New York!
17. Ibid., 235.
18. Ibid.
19. Aiken, *BRPM*, 135.
20. Ibid., 108.
21. Ibid. The term 'moral attitudes' may set off warning sirens, but it merely refers to the sort of attitude expressed in the sentence, 'Would that everyone desired X'.
22. Obviously, brute force and bribery are sometimes effective means of persuasion, at least in the short term. I believe Russell's criteria, once we get to them, usually rule out such means. He also discusses such methods in *Power*, 2nd edition (London: Routledge, 1975); henceforth 'Russell, *Power*'. See Chapters 15 and 17.
23. Bertrand Russell, 'What I Believe', *Why I Am Not a Christian*, ed. Paul Edwards (New York: Simon and Schuster, 1957), 129; henceforth 'Russell, WIB'.
24. Rule-consequentialism is not rule-*based*, though it makes use of rules as general guides for moral decision-making. It is based on the principle of utility.
25. Russell, *RS*, 228.
26. Russell, WIB, 128.
27. Russell, *RS*, 229.
28. Ibid., 231. Russell does not accept this account absolutely, only that it is prima facie true.
29. Ibid. Of course, in such disputes we tend to despise, and thus disparage, those who share our opponents' desires in order to make those desires appear unattractive.
30. Ibid., 232.
31. Though it does not rule out the deceptions of the preacher, should he wish to use them. Russell appears to assume that self-deceptions are bad, though he may characterize them, instead, as destructive and thus a desire for self-deception would probably not be universalizable.
32. Aiken, *BRMP*, 104.
33. Ibid., 105.

34. Russell, *RS*, 235.
35. Ibid., 236.
36. Aiken, *BRPM*, 109.
37. His various accounts of the genealogy and development of different types of ethics and moralities is meant to take care of traditional, bothersome misunderstandings common to moral philosophy, controversies he appears to find philosophically uninteresting.
38. Ibid., 109.
39. Russell, *RS*, 236. Emphasis added.
40. Russell, WIB, 128.
41. Pigden, BR, 502.
42. Yet the way in which he avoids them is similar to what we offered in defence of Ayer and Stevenson.
43. Ibid.
44. Ibid., 133.
45. Ibid., 132.
46. It also indicates that it may be more accurate to refer to Russell's mature emotivism as *non-cognitivism.*
47. We encountered the consequences of such reasoning when we discussed Ayer's and Stevenson's theories.
48. See Russel, *RS*, 239.
49. Ibid., 240.
50. If we are to understand him, we must remember that Russell's metaethics were always matched to a normative theory – usually a form of rule-consequentialism. Thus, one could be obligated to perform an act if it is in the general interests of humanity, even if one does not desire the promotion of those interests (or does not share a desire for them).
51. Ibid., 240–1.
52. Aiken, *BRPM*, 115–6.
53. Russell, *Power*, 169.
54. Ibid., 171.
55. Yes, one may choose not to act on that obligation, but that is true no matter how one conceives of ethics. No matter how moral obligation is conceived, it never involves the transformation of human beings into obedient automatons obligingly meeting every duty.
56. Aiken, *BRPM*, 115. Then again, 'fear of the bad' has a considerable influence as well! Russell is exaggerating. Thanks to Sami Najm for pointing this out.
57. Russell, *RS*, 242–3. I expect he is writing loosely. We should interpret

him as saying that although human beings are naturally self-interested, expanding the sphere of our concern beyond ourselves is not quite the daunting task it may appear to be.

58. Ibid., 241.
59. Ibid., 242.
60. Aiken, *BRPM*, 116.
61. Bertrand Russell, 'Reply to Criticisms', *Collected Papers, Volume 11*, 49–50; henceforth 'Russell, *Reply*'. Russell is using 'objectivity' here in the sense that judgments of fact do not depend in any way on our desires. They are independent of how we feel and what we want.
62. The work of Kuhn, Lakatos *et al* certainly casts doubt on this bold claim.
63. Ibid., 50. Perhaps. Nonetheless, it is obviously not the case that in 'pure' matters of fact, controversies do not last long – astronomers are still debating whether the universe will eventually collapse or expand forever. Thanks to Nick Griffin for the reminder.
64. Ibid.
65. Ibid.
66. Ibid., 50–1. In regard to 'beliefs', Russell is perhaps speaking loosely. To say that I believe murder is wrong is to say that I desire that everyone did not desire to kill others, or something of the sort. We may still use the word 'belief', but its meaning is analyzed in terms of desire.
67. Ibid., 51.
68. Aiken *BRPM*, 142.
69. He appears to imply a similar point in *Religion and Science*, anyway; see *RS*, 242.
70. Pigden, BR, 503.
71. Pigden, *RoE*, 145.
72. Russell, Reply, 48.
73. Ibid.
74. Ibid.
75. Ibid.
76. Ibid., 48–9.
77. The principle here could be expressed as: 'It is irrational to treat A and B differently if there is no relevant difference between them.'
78. Ibid., 49.
79. Pigden, BR, 503.
80. Aiken, *BRPM*, 142. Her Russell references are *RS* 233, 234, 241, and WIB 32.

81. An account of a generally accepted moral standard would be psychology, for Russell – not moral philosophy.
82. Pigden, *RoE*, 135. Another, which I will not consider here, is the old 'But we *believe* we're using ethical propositions' line. Really, Pigden should know better.
83. Ibid., 134. The original objection can be found in Geach's *Logic Matters* (Oxford: Blackwell, 1972), 250–4.
84. Thanks to Nick Griffin for dreaming this up.
85. Aiken, *BRPM*, 151.
86. Russell, Reply, 51.

4

Impulse and Desire

The Path to Integration

At this point the need to know what Russell means by 'desire' imposes itself. Russell had a lot to say about desire early in his career, but he does not appear *consciously* to have incorporated much of that work into his mature metaethic. Consequently, that work has been tragically neglected by those interested in Russell's ethics, leading them to misjudge and misunderstand his theory. In addition, an explicit integration of Russell's theories of desire and impulse into his enlightened emotivism reveals an even more sophisticated theory – one far superior to Stevenson's.

The key to understanding the relationship between Russell's work on desire and his work on ethics is found in Russell's initial motivation for studying desire. He decided to pursue the topic during the First World War – the period in which he became a non-cognitivist. His first serious attempt to analyze and understand the role of desire in human activity was *Principles of Social Reconstruction*, written in 1915.[1] The second, found in *The Analysis of Mind*, was begun while he was in prison for writing an article critical of the use of soldiers as strikebreakers in the United States. During the war, Russell was greatly disturbed and confused by the human drive to inflict suffering, leading him to search for the reasons behind our frequent malevolence, why people act in negative and destructive ways, 'and how they might be persuaded to act positively and creatively', as Kennedy states it.[2]

The point is that he was motivated to study desire and impulse by an ethical concern: the behaviour of human beings toward one another. It would be surprising if this work was irrelevant to an ethical theory that focused on desire, would it not?

Desire as Behaviour

So what does Russell mean by 'desire'? A desire is a longing for that which one does not possess or a state of affairs which does not yet exist. Whether we are aware of them or not, desires are purposive, directed toward the pursuit of an end assumed to be satisfying. They exist in 'an interval of time between the consciousness of a need and the opportunity for satisfying it'.[3] Often, desires lead to suffering – either because of their objects, or because of the time that must elapse before they can be satisfied. And this is where *will* comes in, as a 'directing force' that 'consists mainly in following desires for more or less distant objects, in spite of the painfulness of the acts involved and the solicitations of incompatible but more immediate desires and impulses'.[4]

We could, at this point, attempt to apply Russell's conception of desire to his enlightened emotivism, to test whether his theory works as well as he thought it did. But the situation is more complicated than that theory suggests. For, as important as desire is, its primary purpose is organization – it 'governs no more than a part of human activity, and that not the most important but only the more conscious, explicit, and civilized part'.[5]

Russell is a psychological egoist with idiosyncratic behaviourist tendencies and a modicum of respect for psychoanalysis – we must acknowledge his leanings if we are to properly understand his analysis of desire. He makes it quite clear in *The Analysis of Mind* that we begin to understand which desires motivate people (including ourselves) through careful observation of their actions; since people deceive themselves and others when it comes to the motivations behind their behaviour, observation provides a more reliable way to cut through words in order to discover what is *truly* desired. Although some attention, negative of course, has been paid to his behaviourist tendencies, very little has been paid to his psychological egoism. Yet it is assumed throughout his work, from the earliest stages onward, rising to the surface now and again to colour his premises. By ignoring it, we run the risk of misunderstanding him. By acknowledging it, his work makes a great deal more sense.

For example, we notice after only cursory reflection that Russell's definition of desire *assumes* a weak form of psychological egoism. Desire is recognized in terms of self-interest – in terms of what *I* want, a state of affairs that *I* would like to exist, a longing for something *I* would like to possess. Will is used to control *my* self-interest, to regulate it and keep it from limiting *me* to short-term goals. Perhaps such a definition strikes one as common sense. Yet there is no need to define desire in such terms; it is not necessary. Russell could have specified that some desires are directed toward what others want, what others need, a longing for the satisfaction, say, of one's enemies, even though one would rather see them roasted on a spit. That we have a tendency to think of even those desires in terms of self-interest, one might say, is prima facie evidence in favour of psychological egoism. But that is another matter. The notion of impersonal desires enters the picture in his metaethical writing. And his books on education, especially when read in light of his emotivism and psychological egoism, indicate that he believed that all or most of us begin as self-centred and self-interested, but also that a good education can lead us to develop more inclusive interests. Russell's psychological egoism is a perspective on human nature – but only as regards our initial state, and even then it is not absolute. There are exceptions to the rule, and all or most of us can change our natures to some degree.

As Russell understands it, we are motivated by a sort of discomfort that sets in motion a *behaviour-cycle*, a series of actions beginning with a 'state of activity' consisting of movements believed likely to lead to certain desired results. Such activity continues (unless interrupted by accident, death or another behaviour-cycle)[6] until the desired result is achieved – that is, until a pleasurable state of affairs has been reached – 'usually a period of comparative quiescence'[7] or a comfortable return to the status quo. We call this pleasurable state of affairs the *purpose* of the behaviour-cycle – although our desire need not have been a desire for this state of affairs in particular.

A desire, then, is a state of discomfort that leads one to seek quiescence; it is 'a characteristic of a certain series of actions', namely, those actions commonly regarded as having been inspired by the initial discomfort.[8] Desires that are 'accompanied by a true belief as to the state of affairs that will bring quiescence' Russell calls 'conscious desires'.[9] The rest are unconscious (or perhaps subconscious); 'All primitive desire is unconscious, and in human beings beliefs as to the purposes of desires are often mistaken. These mistaken beliefs generate *secondary desires*, which cause various interesting complications in the psychology of human desire.'[10]

The concept is simple, easy to grasp and to apply. To use a mundane example, when I say that I desire chocolate, I mean that I do not at present have chocolate in my mouth, overwhelming me with rapturous taste-sensations, and I feel a longing for it. My desire is directed toward the end of acquiring chocolate, at which point it will be satisfied. Simple. Were I eating chocolate already, I would no longer desire it – the desire that I once felt would have been satisfied. If my desire for chocolate is attended by a true belief as to how I may satisfy it (I could go to the store, pick a bar off the shelf, and pay a dollar), it is conscious. So my desire sets in motion a behaviour-cycle in which I carry out a plan based on what I believe will lead to the satisfaction of my desire for chocolate. The activity constituting my behaviour-cycle will continue until I have satisfied my desire – unless, that is, something interrupts the activity, such as an accident, my death, someone else's activities or another behaviour-cycle driven by a stronger desire.

Now let us use a particularly ethical example, in order to demonstrate how Russell's theory of desire could be integrated into his enlightened emotivism. To say that 'Peace is good' is to say 'Would that everyone desired peace'. And, if peace is truly good, then it is capable of being *universally desired.* Using Russell's theory of desire we find that 'Would that everyone desired peace' means: 'Would that those who do not yet live in a state of peace, are discomfited by that lack of peace, and who long to live in a state of peace, undertake such action as will create that state of peace'[11] – and, probably: 'Would that those who are actively preventing a state of peace from existing, and who desire ends contrary to a state of peace, desire and act as do those who long for peace.' Furthermore, I expect Russell would like us to be *conscious* of our desire for peace, because a desire that is attended by a true belief as to how we can create a peaceful world is more likely to be satisfied. Our desire would set in motion a behaviour-cycle intended to bring it about. It is obviously a long-term goal though, so most people now living will die before it is ever achieved.

The most problematic aspect of Russell's analysis of desire lies in his odd distinction between conscious and unconscious desires.[12] Surely, we object, a desire can be conscious even when we lack the slightest clue as to how we might bring about quiescence. One may desire to be loved, for instance, and be fully aware of the desire (that is, conscious of it in a customary sense) without having a true belief regarding the conditions for its satisfaction. One may, in fact, have several attendant false beliefs – such as, 'People will love me if I appear needy' – that frustrate one's striving for blissful relief.

Russell attempts to answer the objection indirectly by claiming that we may be mistaken about a *belief's* purpose, 'since only experience can show what causes a discomfort to cease'.[13] In the case of common desires linked to common experiences – such as hunger – mistakes are unlikely. Few sane people would use interpretive dance to satisfy their desire for food. 'But in other cases – e.g. erotic desire in those who have had little or no experience of its satisfaction – mistakes are to be expected, and do in fact very often occur.'[14] Much of the blame should be assigned to our necessary habit of inhibiting impulses, which prevents us from experiencing the satisfaction of certain desires and which hides the inhibited impulses from our attention. These mistakes, Russell insists, 'constitute a large proportion of what is, mistakenly in part, called self-deception, and attributed by Freud to the "censor" '.[15]

When we are conscious of a desire, the motivating discomfort 'belongs to the *belief* that we desire such-and-such a thing that we do not possess'.[16] Consequently, if we are mistaken about the object of our desire, our false belief may generate a 'subsidiary secondary desire' which then becomes real.[17] Thus, a desire that is unconscious (because it is attended by a false belief as to its satisfaction), is unconscious precisely *because* the motivating desire and the desire one believes one has are two different things. One's belief that one has the desire which one does not have may become true, because the belief may *generate* that desire. The primary desire remains unconscious. However:

A secondary desire, derived from a false judgment as to a primary desire, has its own power of influencing action, and is therefore a real desire according to our definition. But it has not the same power as a primary desire of bringing thorough satisfaction when it is realized; so long as the primary desire remains unsatisfied, restlessness continues in spite of the secondary desire's success.[18]

Any quiescence resulting from the satisfaction of a secondary desire will be superficial unless the primary desire from which it arose is satisfied. Beneath illusory satisfaction lies lingering unease.

But there is a difference between having an unconscious desire and, say, settling for the near-satisfaction brought about by a substitute. Suppose I have a genuine desire for chocolate ice cream but despite my best efforts I am unable to find any. Frustrated, I settle for vanilla as a substitute. I did not have an unconscious desire for vanilla ice cream, but it was the only ice cream available. Russell does not seem to allow for this sort of situation, which prevents his theory from being wholly adequate until an apologist steps in with a suitably 'Russellian' solution.

Regarding our claim that a desire to be loved may be conscious even when attended by several false beliefs, Russell would agree that the beliefs are false but he would still insist that the desire must be unconscious. Not only is that an unlikely story, we simply have no compelling reason to believe that the consciousness of a desire must be accompanied by a true belief about how to satisfy it. There is no necessary connection. Because of that absent necessary connection, our claim that some conscious desires may not be attended by *any* beliefs still appears to stand, with one exception: the belief that one lacks what one desires. Are we to believe that the desire to be loved felt by some poor outcast who has never had any experience of love, and so has no beliefs regarding possible courses for satisfaction, is unconscious *because* he lacks those beliefs? I think, on the other hand, that the chap would be quite aware of his frustrating desire, beliefs aside. Furthermore, his desire may lead him into certain kinds of activity, perhaps intended to distract him from that very desire (*not* satisfy it), although I am prepared to accept that this is not what Russell refers to as a 'behaviour-cycle'. We may let him define his specialized terms as he wishes, but his failure to provide precise criteria for applying the term and distinguishing one behaviour-cycle from another will come back to haunt him.

We could modify Russell's theory to allow that a desire may be unconscious if it is fictitious, that is, accompanied by false beliefs regarding what would satisfy it, or by no beliefs at all (because one does not really have the desire). His assertion that a *conscious* desire must be accompanied by a true belief as to the means to its satisfaction may, then, apply only to genuine desires – or derivative desires compatible with their instinctive source and not involving any deception. By adjusting his theory in this way, I believe, it becomes acceptable. He still has not given us a reason to believe in any necessary connection between genuine desires and true beliefs, but his claim becomes more plausible than it was.

Impulse and the Principle of Growth

Desire and *impulse* are the twin motivations of human activity, according to Russell, but the latter is far more significant. The distinction between desires and impulses is crucial, and not all that obvious at first; at times even Russell appears to get them confused. In those works in which he set out his theory of enlightened emotivism, he appears to have neglected impulse entirely.[19] By correcting this mistake, we can strengthen his theory – making it more consistent with his analyses of desire and impulse, and making his enlightened emotivism more sophisticated.

Why do we not realize how powerfully, and how often, we are motivated by desire and impulse? Russell finds the answer in the insights of psychoanalysis, which he believes has demonstrated that the causes of our actions, desires and emotions are often hidden from us, buried somewhere in the subconscious, or simply ignored. And these insights would make much more sense, he believes, if translated into behaviouristic terms.[20] In *Principles of Social Reconstruction*, Russell spends far more time analyzing impulse than desire. He considers impulse our primary motivation. Even our beliefs, he argues, 'are, in the main, a product of instinct and circumstance'.[21] Yet we tend to suppress our impulses because they are 'erratic and anarchical, not easily fitted into a well-regulated system' – hence desire's task of organization. Although we tolerate impulse, to a degree, in children and artists, most adults are expected to ignore such an uncivilized force.

In the so-called 'civilized' world, most of an adult's waking hours are spent in the pursuit of money, and 'Almost all paid work is done from desire . . . the work itself is more or less irksome, but the payment for it is desired.'[22] Thus desire, though it is secondary to impulse, dominates in the civilized world. Nevertheless, our *instinctive* nature is dominated by impulses, directed not toward satisfaction of ends, as desires are, but toward certain types of activity. Although impulses sometimes lead to pleasant consequences, often they do not; it makes no difference, for we are not motivated toward instinctive acts by an appraisal of their probable consequences. It is sheer impulse 'that prompts such actions as eating, drinking, love-making, quarrelling, boasting'.[23] There is no instrumental reasoning at work, contrary to popular belief. Russell explains: 'Those who believe that man is a rational animal will say that people boast in order that others may have a good opinion of them; but most of us can recall occasions when we have boasted in spite of knowing that we should be despised for it.'[24]

Adults also tend to suppress their natural impulses because they are taught to believe human beings are rational, that rationality sets us apart from beasts. Impulses are thought of as, in a sense, bothersome reminders of our 'primitive' ancestry. So we set out to convince ourselves that we are rational, unaware that impulse will not be so easily thwarted. Russell writes:

> When an impulse is not indulged in the moment in which it arises there grows up a desire for the expected consequences of indulging the impulse. If some of the consequences which are reasonably to be expected are clearly disagreeable, a conflict between foresight and impulse arises. If the impulse is weak, foresight may conquer; this is what is called acting on reason. If the impulse is strong, either foresight will be falsified, and the disagreeable consequences will be forgotten, or, in men of a heroic mould, the consequences may be recklessly accepted.[25]

Most impulses are not so strong and reckless – because there is no need. If an impulse is strong enough, we can generally deceive ourselves into believing that giving in to it will lead to pleasant consequences. Such is the power of rationalization. We have, here, the origin of many moral codes and philosophies – the natural result of subconscious subservience to impulse, attempts to rationalize indulgence. As Russell understands it: 'most of what passes for thought is inspired by some non-intellectual impulse, and is merely a means of persuading ourselves that we shall not be disappointed or do harm if we indulge this impulse'.[26]

Impulse, then, plays a larger role in our lives than desire – yet we tend to assume the opposite. Why? The role of desire may be exaggerated *because* of impulse: 'Impulses bring with them a whole train of subservient fictitious desires: they make men feel that they desire the results which will follow from indulging the impulses, and that they are acting for the sake of these results.'[27] Direct impulse is the primary source of human activity, but it often disguises itself, or *we* disguise it in our self-deceptive efforts to retain the conviction that we are somehow above such base motivation.

Russell divides impulses into two categories: creative and possessive. Among the former he includes impulses toward art and science – *civilized* impulses – that is, those directed toward creating something new. Possessive impulses, conversely, are those directed toward the acquisition and retention of what already exists. 'The typical creative impulse', Russell explains, 'is that of the artist; the typical possessive impulse is that of property. The best life [the life inspired by love and guided by knowledge] is that in which creative impulses play the largest part and possessive impulses the smallest.'[28] As he explains in *The Scientific Outlook*, those who seek power – really a set of activities driven by a possessive impulse – can never be satisfied, so the impulse leads to continual disappointment. Yet it continues to work its influence, driving its slaves to seek greater power in the false hope that the end will finally be realized. Creative impulses – such as those which motivate lovers, mystics and poets – bring satisfaction, since the objects of their impulses are not things to be acquired or retained. The satisfaction exists in the very impulse; it is, in a sense, its own object. 'I think, therefore,' Russell concludes, 'that the satisfactions of the lover, using the word in its broadest sense, exceed the satisfactions of the tyrant, and deserve a higher place among the ends of life.'[29] As goods, 'the satisfactions of the lover' are ranked above 'the satisfactions of a tyrant' because, in part, we are *much* more likely to achieve them.

Possessive impulses, to classify further, may be aggressive (intended to acquire) or defensive (intended to retain). The defensive variety of possessive impulses can be rather benign. Yet, although they are preferable to their counterpart, they should be minimized; 'indeed, as soon as they are strong they become hostile to the creative impulses'.[30] One who allows her defensive possessive impulses to flourish and multiply becomes preoccupied with protecting her possessions (even such non-material possessions as knowledge), and is led into a life progressively devoid of creativity and freedom. Some degree of defensive possessiveness is unavoidable, but it must be carefully controlled and minimized, for, possession necessarily involves thwarting the enjoyment of others, whereas creation involves giving something new to the world, for the enjoyment of oneself and others.[31] The two are often incompatible.

We have now a small hierarchy of psychological forces relevant to ethics, with impulse ranked higher than desire in terms of significance and influence. Yet, behind all impulses and desires lurks *the principle of growth*, 'an instinctive urgency leading them in a certain direction, as trees seek the light'.[32] Central to every person's being, the principle of growth differs from one to another, 'and determines for each man the type of excellence of which he is capable'.[33] Social institutions could –*should* – be such as are able to help all people progress to their utmost potential (what might now be called 'self-realization'), toward which the principle of growth directs them. Russell believes that the greater the degree of self-realization in each person, the greater the degree of universal harmony.

The point of requiring social institutions to promote the principle of growth is to prevent problems arising from its impediment. When the principle is thwarted, impulses become perverted – and those that develop out of thwarted growth, such as impulses toward drug-taking or cruel behaviour, can be dangerous; they should be kept in check by self-discipline, what Russell calls 'inward will'. The outlets an impulse is habitually allowed to use determine which of a variety of forms that impulse will take – an impulse that leads to artistic expression in one may lead to warmongering in another. Even some impulses that stem directly from the principle may sometimes lead to harm.[34]

One may object that we have no reason to expect that the degree of universal harmony will increase if the degree of self-realization of all people increases. Why should we expect compossibility between self-realizations? After all, until the later stages of the Second World War, Hitler seemed to be one of the most self-realized people in history. Russell would disagree. His answer, I believe, would be that the principle of growth naturally directs us toward creative impulses, and creative impulses are the ones that bring self-realization. The sort of cruel behaviour of which Hitler has become a symbol is a result of a thwarted principle of growth; there is no self-realization to be found there. Such people are full of possessive impulses and fictitious desires. The creative impulses that lead to self-realization are necessarily compossible with one another – compossibility is built in to the very nature of creative impulses. I would not find such a reply very convincing, but I can imagine Russell offering it.

We come, then, to the relation of impulse and desire to ethics. Already we have noted that Russell was motivated to analyze desire and impulse out of a desire to find a way to lead people out of cruelty. Cruelty and suffering, then, Russell considers bad. This is obvious throughout *Principles of Social Reconstruction* and all of his ethical, political and autobiographical writing. Possessive impulses are discouraged, in part, because they prevent others from enjoying things, a low-level sort of cruelty that leads others to suffer. So Russell believes we must exercise self-discipline to a degree necessary to prevent ourselves from indulging in impulses that lead to cruelty, both out of self-interest and out of regard for the interests of others.[35]

How, using Russell's theory, can we make sense of the notion of cruelty and suffering as 'bad'? How can we justify requiring people not to indulge impulses that will lead to the suffering of others? Desires for cruelty and suffering, Russell would argue, are not universalizable. We cannot exclaim, 'Would that everyone desired cruelty and suffering', because such a desire, if realized, is not compossible with desires, say, for happiness and peace, which *are* universalizable.[36] We could say, then, that such desires are morally wrong because, if realized, they would lead to disharmony. That much I am prepared to grant Russell.

But could we say that *cruelty and suffering* are themselves bad, as Russell assumes they are? What would make them so? If to say something is good is to say 'Would that everyone desired this', then we may infer that to say something is bad is to say, 'Would that no one desired this'.[37] If we understand Russell's emotivism in this way, it seems reasonable to call suffering and cruelty bad. At the very least, we can understand why *Russell* feels justified in assuming as much. So, by calling cruelty and suffering bad, Russell is merely expressing his desire that no one desire cruelty and suffering. He has this desire, presumably, because cruelty and suffering conflict with his self-interest. Since they also conflict with *everyone's* self-interest to some extent at some times, he can safely assume that the expressed desire is universal.[38] And because a desire for cruelty and suffering could not be harmonized with the general collective desires of humanity, he believes we would be justified in persuading others to curb such desires, should they have them.

Obviously, Russell considers creative impulses good and possessive impulses (to greater and lesser degrees) bad – this fact is implied in the connotations of the very names he gives them. A life dominated by creative impulses, the artist's, is better than the life of a land baron, dominated by possessive impulses. The *best* life is one in which there is a far greater preponderance of creative impulses over possessive. And hostility toward creative impulses, exemplified in his account by a life of possessiveness, is bad because it leads to less freedom and creativity, both of which he considers good. Such assumptions do not appear contentious once interpreted: it is reasonable to assume that desires for creativity and freedom are either universal or universalizable – one person's act of creation does not hinder another's.[39] Creative impulses do not themselves lead to conflict; turmoil emerges only when possessive impulses infect a situation.

What if two people wishing to indulge their creative impulses needed the same raw materials? Would that not lead to conflict? Russell would argue that impulses do not exist alone, but rather as part of vast collections of impulses and desires within individuals. Other creative impulses and universalizable desires would prevent conflict between 'good' people in such situations. Furthermore, in this case there are clearly possessive impulses at work, and these are the impulses that lead to conflict. Still, we could conclude that in some cases, certain creative impulses may be necessarily (or perhaps only 'usually') connected to certain possessive impulses. A bigger problem may come from the creative impulse to destroy. Perhaps one has an impulse to create chaos and disorder. One would expect such an impulse to lead someone into conflict with others quite frequently. To this suggestion Russell would reply that such an impulse is obviously the result of a thwarted principle of growth. Recall his contention that the same impulse that leads one to become an artist may lead another to become a warmonger. The difference lies in the outlets habitually given to the impulse. A creative impulse toward destruction may be a perverted creative impulse that might have otherwise led the destructive person to paint pictures of butterflies and dancing children. So yes, Russell might agree, in this case a creative impulse can lead to conflict – but it has become perverted by a thwarted principle of growth.

The overall practicality of Russell's theory is manifest in his account of 'good relations'. Good relations between individuals are based on the sense of a common purpose – in particular, one that requires co-operation with others in order to be realized – and 'instinctive liking', out of which a sense of common purpose may develop. 'Instinctive liking', he explains, 'is the feeling which makes us take pleasure in another person's company, find an exhilaration in his presence, wish to talk with him, work with him, play with him'.[40] The degree of instinctive liking present in individuals varies greatly – it even varies within an individual at different moments. Some people instinctively like everyone, some instinctively dislike everyone, most lie somewhere between the two extremes. No objective reasons can be levied to prove that any of these attitudes is more *rational* than the others. 'If a man finds people repulsive,' Russell claims, 'no argument can prove to him that they are not so. But both his own desires and other people's are more likely to find satisfaction' if he instinctively likes most people.[41] A world full of such people would be much happier than our present world, or a world of the opposite extreme. Would that there were more instinctive liking in the world!

But when it comes to the principle of growth, Russell appears to stumble. He assumes, apparently, that the principle of growth is both an intrinsic and an instrumental good, leading to *other* intrinsic goods[42] – such as personal excellence, i.e., realization of potential – unless it is thwarted in some way. Social institutions ought to allow the principle of growth to operate unimpeded for precisely this reason.

> When a man's growth is unimpeded, his self-respect remains intact, and he is not inclined to regard others as his enemies. But when, for whatever reason, his growth is impeded, or he is compelled to grow into some twisted and unnatural shape, his instinct presents the environment as his enemy, and he becomes filled with hatred. The joy of life abandons him, and malevolence takes the place of friendliness. . . . Real freedom, if it could be brought about, would go a long way towards destroying hatred.[43]

The greater the freedom available to people, the less impeded the principle of growth.

How can Russell argue that the principle of growth is an *intrinsic* good? It is the source of creativity, yes, and is to be valued on that account. Yet to say 'Would that everyone desired the principle of growth' makes little sense. What is it, precisely, that is being desired? A principle that leads to creativity and the realization of potential? What is desired is not the principle itself, it seems, but creativity and self-realization, both of which can be had without a principle to drive us toward them. The principle of growth may exist – though Russell offers no evidence that it is anything but a theoretical construct – but his theory cannot make sense of it as an intrinsic good, which Russell clearly assumes it is. On the other hand, if Russell considers *growth itself* intrinsically good, I am prepared to grant him that, for the moment.[44]

Russell's consequentialism pervades his work on desire and impulse. For example, we ought to exercise self-control, even if it is painful, in order to prevent desires for short-term goals from hindering the realization of more significant long-term goals. The consequences of exercising such self-control are better than the consequences of seeking short-term gratification. And we are to take great care when suppressing impulses because doing so leads primarily to self-deception, which Russell assumes is a bad consequence (and which he also believes is less common than we tend to assume).[45] In this case, I would interpret Russell not as claiming that *self-deception* itself is bad, but that it leads to bad consequences, such as the distortion of impulses into harmful forms. Eventually, I expect, suffering and delusion result – as they eventually do from most false beliefs (though not all). On the other hand, self-deception may also lead to happiness, as Kierkegaard and James believe.

No matter. Russell's theory could also make sense of the notion that self-deception itself is bad. 'Would that everyone desired to deceive herself' is not likely to be universalizable and is contrary to the second of Russell's criteria of the good life.

Self-deception is not guided by knowledge, nor by a desire for knowledge, but by ignorance and a desire to avoid knowledge.

But, given his consequentialism, is it not significant that impulses pay no attention whatsoever to ends? If the consequences of some impulses are sometimes pleasant, as Russell suggests, are they good? Creative impulses, he admits, do not always lead to desirable consequences and possessive impulses do not always lead to undesirable consequences. Yet he wishes to make blanket statements regarding them: creative impulses are good, possessive impulses are bad – to varying degrees. Perhaps he may feel justified in such generalizations because, say, creative impulses have a *tendency* to lead to desirable ends. The explanation may lie in Russell's normative ethics. If he is a rule-utilitarian, or rule-consequentialist, as he often appears to be, his generalization may fit into a pattern of thought. Because creative impulses tend to lead to results that we desire we may say that they are good, and as a general rule that we ought to promote them over their possessive counterparts – vice versa for possessive impulses. This makes for a reasonable interpretation of Russell, I believe, and one consistent with his enlightened emotivism.

Confusing Consequences

To summarize, impulses are involved in moral activity in the following manner: a universalizable desire for peace, for instance, may be inspired by a creative impulse toward peace-making activity. If the principle of growth inspires one toward such activity, then it is part of what will bring one closer to personal excellence. Surely, if this is the case, peace-lovers are to be desired. Optimally, all of one's impulses will be of this sort, compatible with the general desires of humanity, leading one toward universal desires. And because creative impulses are capable of mutual satisfaction, and because they tend to lead to generally desired consequences, we may call them 'good'.

What about the problems Russell faces in relation to his concept of conscious desires? Do they arise in relation to impulses? Whether Russell truly believes that all desires stemming from impulses are fictitious secondary desires, intended to hide their source by throwing out red herrings, is unclear. If so, that may be due to the fact that impulses do not take ends into account, whereas desires do. So a desire that stems from an impulse, since it is a desire *for* something, for an end, must be fictitious *if* it merely serves to mask an impulse. It may be the case that an impulse could bring about a complementary desire, not a fictitious one – a desire that does not serve to hide an impulse, but rather is directed toward ends compatible with the activity driven by the impulse. For example, a creative impulse toward peace-making activity may lead to a desire for peace that is not at all fictitious and serves, rather, to give purpose to the inevitable end of *successful* peace-making activity. Recall the behaviouristic aspects of Russell's theory of desire. He is forced to define desires by the end result of their behaviour-cycles in order to avoid identifying them by their objects.

It is this aspect that invited Wittgenstein's famous objection: if a behaviour-cycle inspired by a desire for chocolate is ended by, say, a punch to the stomach, should we not say, according to Russell's theory, that it is the punch to the stomach that one desired? Russell's response would be that the cycle was interrupted; it did not achieve its purpose. The actions involved in the behaviour-cycle in question are not likely to be those expected if the desire was for a punch to the stomach. On the other hand, they make sense if one desired chocolate. We can determine what was desired in the case of an interrupted behaviour-cycle by paying close attention to the constitutive actions. However, this will not *always* be possible: many actions, even their sequences, are shared by different behaviour-cycles.

Until the purpose of a behaviour-cycle has been realized, determining which desire is operative is not an easy task. Does sex mask an unconscious desire for cigarettes?[46] How do we know when one behaviour-cycle ends and another begins unless we know what the operative desire is *before* it is satisfied?

Perhaps we are being too narrow. I expect Russell would urge us to think in more general terms. A desire for sex and a desire for cigarettes are both, in more general terms, desires for pleasure – and perhaps it does not matter which path we take to satisfy this general desire. The pop-psychologists paraded out on talk shows like to talk about, for example, an extraordinarily strong desire for food as a mask for unconscious desires for attention, company, comfort, etc. Might it not be the case that people desire happiness (and/or pleasure), and that this desire can lead to any number of behaviour-cycles? It may be satisfied when one eats, or enjoys pleasant company, or is praised, or feels secure, and so forth. Perhaps, even, each of these ends satisfies the desire to a different degree, so that when the 'purpose' has been achieved, one may still feel the desire. If we took each of these ends as the 'purpose' of the behaviour-cycle – that is, as the operative desire – we mislead ourselves. The question we need to ask is: 'What benefit does someone get from this end?' Once we have answered that question, we can abstract it into a desire, find other ends that indicate the same desire, and organize desires in classes. To think in this way is consistent with Russell's con-sequentialist and psychological egoist inclinations.

However, when we do this we come to realize that there are no absolutely distinct behaviour-cycles; they are not organized in a chain-like sequence of desires X, Y, and Z. We find instead multiple sequences of behaviour-cycles, overlapping at various points, and resembling an interwoven series of sequences – a long piece of chain mail rather than a chain. At any given time, one will be involved in multiple behaviour-cycles that will end with the satisfaction (complete or partial) of multiple desires. In many (perhaps most) cases, the same series of actions is involved in several different behaviour-cycles as well – human beings rarely do anything for just one reason. For example, someone who buys a house may do so because she desires to own her place of residence, because she desires to invest in property that she may cash in on at some later date, and because she desires the status that a house in a wealthy neighbourhood will bring. We have three convergent desires here – all consisting of more-or-less the same actions constituting what amounts to the same behaviour-cycle, all of which will likely be satisfied at the same time. Russell's commitment to behaviourism turns this into a problem. If he must identify desires by the termination-points of their behaviour-cycles, then he needs to be able to clearly distinguish one behaviour-cycle from another *without* using intentional descriptions, *without* slipping into the habit of identifying desires by their objects. He cannot. We cannot know, in most cases, which desire is operative in any given behaviour-cycle until it ends. But we cannot even tell, with any accuracy, when a behaviour-cycle has ended, because it is blended with so many others. When cycle A ends, others begin – others ended just before A, more will end just after A, some ended halfway through A, and most of them probably shared many of their constitutive actions. Russell needs to revert to the identification of desires by their objects. Later in life, thankfully, he appeared to understand the bankruptcy of behaviourism.

On a related note, a confusion of impulses with desire pervades Russell's theory. Take sex, which we have recently spoken of in terms of desire – one has a desire *for* sexual activity, which we call 'lust'. Yet Russell treats it as an impulse. Which is it? If it is a desire, it will be satisfied at the termination of a behaviour-cycle. If it is a conscious desire, it will be accompanied by a true belief as to what will bring quiescence to that state of discomfort, the state of longing for what one does not have. Lust does terminate momentarily at the completion of a behaviour-cycle, and once one reaches a certain age, or experience level, one's lust is accompanied by true beliefs as to what will satisfy it. Yet it also appears to be an impulse, since it is satisfied by an *activity* as well, by the behaviour-cycle itself. One may look at it either way, as an impulse or as a desire. Russell's theory does not give us any way to determine which it is, nor does it specify whether something can be both an impulse *and* a desire. I expect that, in a case such as this, we could define lust as both an impulse toward an activity and as a desire that will be satisfied once we have reached the end of that activity.

Yet we still ask ourselves, 'What is it a desire for?' – which implies an object. Perhaps Russell might say that we think this way because we are accustomed to thinking of desires in terms of their objects, which, at this point, he still believes is illicit.

Bases of Disagreement

Russell's account of ethical debate is more interesting in *Principles of Social Reconstruction* than in his later books on ethics proper. Here he writes that we tend not to understand impulses we do not share (or cannot share vicariously, through imagination). So, when we confront someone moved to activity by impulses different from our own, we come to different conclusions regarding the ends of that activity, and their desirability. In *The Analysis of Mind,* he characterizes this sort of dispute as follows:[47] Albert states that he has a desire for justice, and this desire has led him to take part in rallies, protests and letter-writing campaigns. But Bertha 'perceives' that Albert's actions will lead to much 'different ends' than those Albert claims to desire – to, say, a small measure of local fame and the adulation of female activists. Thus, Bertha concludes that it is reasonable to attribute to Albert desires for fame and female admiration. Since desires for these ends are not considered as admirable as a desire for justice, we would expect Albert not to publicly profess them – so Bertha concludes that Albert has an impulse to be recognized and admired, which he will not admit to himself (perhaps because he wants to maintain a conventionally virtuous self-image), or others (for a similar reason).

Albert may actually have an impulse to help others, and this impulse may be the source of his activity. Because Bertha does not share that impulse, she interprets Albert's actions according to the impulses she feels and understands, which she believes are undesirable.[48] In order to maintain our self-deception, we may create an attendant system of false beliefs. For example, Russell writes:

> we have an impulse to inflict pain on those whom we hate; we therefore believe that they are wicked, and that punishment will reform them. This belief enables us to act upon the impulse to inflict pain, while believing that we are acting on the desire to lead sinners to repentance. It is for this reason that the criminal law has been in all ages more severe then it would have been if the impulse to ameliorate the criminal had been what really inspired it.[49]

Russell does not believe that self-deception explains this phenomenon, since we are too ignorant to require it. To wit: 'Most people, in thinking about punishment, have had no more need to hide their vindictive impulses from themselves than they have had to hide the exponential theorem.'[50] Because we are not always aware of our impulses, we do not always need to hide them from ourselves.

Although the basis of the resulting difference of opinion is simply one of differing impulses, we tend to believe it is 'ethical or intellectual'. When we speak of 'ethical disagreements', we are referring to disagreements between various impulses and desires. So long as we continue to have different impulses, we will not come to any agreement. This is not, in itself, a regrettable fact of life. We need not invent new ways to solve such disagreements and rid ourselves of mad, blind impulse. Yes, 'blind impulses' sometimes lead to destruction and suffering, but they also lead to things of great value, such as science and love. '*It is not the weakening of impulse that is to be desired, but the direction of impulse towards life and growth rather than towards death and decay.*'[51]

There appears to be some inconsistency in this account, for, if impulses are not directed toward ends, how can we speak of having different conclusions regarding the ends of the activity to which they lead? Activity, recall, is the sole end of impulses; impulsive activities are their own ends. But in contradicting himself on this point, if that is what he has done,[52] Russell's account of impulses can become more convincing, for surely impulses do appear to have ends – recall our earlier frustration with lust. The end of eating (an activity caused by an impulse) is the cessation of hunger, say, and the end of sex is pleasure or the temporary cessation of lust. Each impulse necessarily has a corresponding desire, regardless of whether we are conscious of it. The impulse toward eating is paired with a desire for the cessation of hunger, and the impulse toward sex is matched with a desire for the cessation of lust – perhaps both also involve a secondary desire for pleasure. Or, perhaps, the desire for pleasure may simply be the governing desire, if we consider these matters on a more general level.

So how are we to make sense of Russell's account of ethical disputes? Perhaps in an ethical disagreement over capital punishment, Albert feels an impulse toward vengeful activity. That impulse leads him to desire a feeling of justice having been done, of metaphorical scales having been balanced. The impulse is possessive, in that it is directed toward the acquisition of something Albert does not have – a state of justice in the world, or a feeling that justice has been done. Bertha, on the other hand, feels an impulse toward life-preserving activity, and thus a desire for a state of affairs that does not yet exist, say, benevolence in the penal system. Her impulse is creative. Each, presumably, interprets the end of the other's activity as undesirable. 'Would that no one desired peace for convicts!' Albert might say. 'Would that no one desired bloodthirsty vengeance!' responds Bertha. Until each shares the other's impulse, they will not come to any agreement.

But is it really the case that all we have here is a difference of impulses and desires? Is there really no 'ethical or intellectual' disagreement, as Russell maintains? Presumably, by 'ethical disagreement', Russell means the 'traditional' view of ethical disagreements, in which there are ethical facts to be known. We will grant him that. However, what does it mean to say there is no 'intellectual' disagreement? Does he mean that there are no facts – ethical or otherwise – in dispute? If so, he is mistaken. Both parties may have an arsenal of facts at their disposal. Albert may give reasons why, say, murderers should be executed; perhaps recidivism statistics and the old deterrence card. This would be a practical matter – 'should' in this case having a meaning similar to that used in, 'You should wear a helmet when riding your bicycle'. Bertha, on the other hand, may cite similar facts regarding the possibility of wrongful conviction: if the executed person is not the true culprit, then execution does not accomplish its goal, instead it accomplishes a great deal of what both Albert and Bertha would likely regard as harm.

That there is an intellectual component to such disagreements is clear. Russell himself suggests that there may be facts relevant to ethical matters, and that such facts may be used to persuade someone to change her position by leading her to reclassify an action. The conclusion to be drawn, I suggest, is that although ethical disagreements may be rooted in a difference of impulse, they may also be rooted in facts, selected and interpreted in various ways. Russell's theory can make sense of this conclusion, for facts must always be interpreted. Impulses and desires sometimes lead to rationalization and self-deception. It is a short step to the contention that they colour our perceptions and interpretations more generally, that the way in which we interpret data is always affected by our impulses and desires. So, although there may be an intellectual component to ethical disagreement, it is filtered through our impulses and desires in such a way that we can claim that they are the ultimate basis of ethical disagreement.

Creating Desires and Impulses

Despite the primacy of impulse and desire in ethical disputes, Russell contends that we should seek not to control these forces with massive amounts of will power, but rather alter them through education. He realizes many will find such a contention odd, for moralists stereotypically preach slogans of will power, self-control and the like. But, he claims, any life which attempts to use will to exclude impulse, leaving purpose and desire to govern, is tiring, exhausting and in the end leads to general indifference. It is a dull life, all the excitement and pleasure having been sucked away.[53] Later he writes, 'Impulse is the expression of life, and while it exists there is hope of its turning towards life instead of death; but lack of impulse is death, and out of death no new life will come.'[54] That's a lovely claim, a terrifically quotable sentence, but what does he mean?

The Industrial Revolution, Russell claims, with its shrill and narrow focus on purpose, turned entire nations into feeble shells of what they once were, left unable to realize their desires.[55] In time such a life leads to the creation of new impulses which the will has not been trained to control, and of which one may not be conscious. Such impulses lead to destructive and cruel activity because their very creation involved thwarting the principle of growth.[56] Our natural and spontaneous impulses must have an outlet. One might object that some impulses are too dangerous not to control. But we do not have a fixed set of specific impulses, issued at birth, unchanged throughout our lives. We need not accept our natural instincts as simply there, given, forces to be accepted as fixed and inevitable. Each of us has a certain natural disposition, with its own inclinations and tendencies, 'which co-operates with outside circumstances in producing a certain character. But even the instinctive part of our nature is very malleable. It may be changed by beliefs, by material circumstances, by social circumstances, and by institutions such as schools.[57] Education was Russell's goal in many of his most popular books: *The Conquest of Happiness, Education and the Social Order* and *Religion and Science*, to name but a few.

Will, nonetheless, is valuable. Russell divides it into two types: one directed outward, the other inward. Outward will becomes necessary when one encounters external obstacles, be they environmental, technical or interpersonal.[58] This sort 'is an expression of strong impulse or desire, whenever instant success is impossible; it exists in all whose life is vigorous, and only decays when their vital force is enfeebled'.[59] Such will is necessary for any great success in life. On the other hand, inward will is necessary only to resolve internal conflicts of desire and impulse – ideally, we seek inner harmony to relieve the necessity of inward will.[60] Although no one actually possesses complete inner harmony, it is an ideal we should attempt to approximate to the greatest extent possible – the closer we come to perfect inner harmony, the fewer incompatible impulses waging war within us, the happier we will be. After all, the expenditure of energy on using will to keep impulses in check diminishes our vitality, distracts us from occasions requiring outward will, and diverts controlled impulses into twisted subterranean paths. 'For these reasons,' Russell concludes, 'the necessity for using inward will ought to be avoided as much as possible, and consistency of action ought to spring rather from consistency of impulse than from control of impulse by will.'[61] A primary, and quite practical, goal of education, then, should be the creation of *harmonious* desires and impulses to the greatest possible degree.

Russell appears to believe that will power may be used to control the *strength* of our desires in conjunction with indirect controls, such as controlling one's circumstances and environment. Our circumstances and environments affect our impulses and desires, and hence our actions. Thus, when someone tells us, 'You ought to do X', we will do X if and only if we desire to do X (or desire the end which X will help us realize) – or if the speaker, or society, approves of it.[62] Here 'good' acts as a force for social cohesion, its power dependent on our desire for social approval and fear of disapproval.

More interesting, though, is that Russell spends very little time dealing with the strength of desires. His definition of 'desire' requires that any strong desire is acted upon, and that makes sense. However, his theory appears to be incapable of accounting for any desires that we do not act upon, because they are not exhibited by behaviour-cycles. The suggestion that we act upon every desire that we have is absurd, and Russell does not make it: he believes we can choose not to act on desires (at least, those that are conscious). Yet his theory appears to require the opposite. If someone chooses not to act on a desire, then how can we say she has that desire unless we revert to identifying it in terms of its object? In Chapter 3 we noted that Russell did not mention whether the strength of a given desire, compared to others, was relevant to moral judgments and decisions. Now the answer is clear, though unsatisfactory: no. Weak desires do not matter because, using Russell's conception of a desire, they do not exist. Now, if we are using 'weak' in a relative sense – say, to speak of a strong desire that is weaker than another strong desire, though both lead to behaviour-cycles – then the strength of a desire is irrelevant. All that matters is whether a desire is universalizable and compossible with other universal desires – inspired by love and guided by knowledge.

Although creative and possessive impulses are *moral* opposites, *psychologically* one may be transformed into the other, 'according to accidents of circumstance and opportunity'.[63] We must remain on guard, for we have already discovered the effect that suppressed desires, a thwarted principle of growth, self-deception and rationalization can have on impulses and desires. Education can help us prevent the transformation of creative impulses into possessive, and promote the converse. It can, indeed should, be used to strengthen harmonious impulses and weaken the others, leading to a greater balance of good over bad.

To what extent, if any, can *reason* affect our desires and impulses? Hume's influence on Russell is obvious, particularly in *Principles of Social Reconstruction*. Russell writes that, if more people were rational, they would agree that war is self-destructive foolishness, that the reasons against it far outweigh the reasons in its favour. However, reason and unclouded thought are insufficient. We overestimate the degree to which we are moti-vated by reason, by rational deliberation, by beliefs. Only those for whom the desire to think truly has the intensity of a passion will be so motivated – since passions, impulses and desires can only be controlled by their kin.[64] Indeed, reason is necessary for peace, but it must be accompanied by 'a positive life of impulses and passions antagonistic to those that lead to war. *It is the life of impulse that needs to be changed, not only the life of conscious thought.*'[65]

All right, not *only* the life of conscious thought needs to be changed. But in what way does it need to be changed? And, if we are motivated primarily by impulse and desire, to what extent does reason matter? Russell's answers to these questions are frustratingly elusive. Aiken notes that at times he appears to conceive of reason as a tool of desire, an instrument to be used at desire's reckoning, as does Hume – indeed, sometimes Russell appears to agree entirely with Hume.[66] But, at other times, Russell permits reason the power to change our desires.

Related to the issue of reason is that of belief. Later in life, in *Human Society in Ethics and Politics,* Russell wrote: 'If moral "beliefs", unlike genuine beliefs, motivate, this must be because to "believe" a moral judgment is not to assent to a proposition but to adopt a desire or register an emotion.'[67] Here he writes that reason – instrumental reason – is concerned only with choosing effective means to an end, not with ends themselves. So, 'Desires, emotions, passions . . . are the only possible causes of action. Reason is not a cause of action but only a regulator.'[68] For instance, although you may believe that execution is an effective deterrent, if you are honest you will not advocate the position unless you actually care about deterrence.

Our desires may also be changed by the connotations we attach to the word 'good'. Russell claims that 'the laudatory associations of the word good may generate a desire which would not otherwise exist: we may want to eat caviar merely because we are told that it is good'.[69] Although in this instance, Russell uses the word 'good' equivocally – first in reference to ethics, second in reference to the quality of a food – I believe he wishes the claim to apply to 'good' in its moral sense. Although I do not find the point confusing, Aiken does. There are two possible interpretations, she proposes. First, when someone says, 'X is good', the word 'good' creates within us desires that we did not previously have because we have an idea of what 'good' means. The speaker desires that everyone desire X, which leads us to desire that everyone desire X.[70] Second, Russell's claim may be that the word 'good' has an 'independent emotive meaning' which immediately brings out our desires and approval – behaviouristically.[71] In her opinion, Russell's use of the word 'laudatory' implies the latter, an interpretation she believes is supported in some of his other books. She writes, 'it seems fairly evident that Russell recognized the importance of the non-cognitive use of words such as "good" and "reality"".[72] In certain contexts, these words function in a purely emotive manner, independent of any descriptive meaning they might have in other contexts.

Aiken has unnecessarily divided Russell's intended meaning into two exclusive interpretations. We need to ask *why* a word such as 'good' would have any behaviouristic effect on us. Russell would have said it was *because* we attach a certain meaning and connotation to the word. The connotation is emotive and, far from being 'independent', it is actually connected with the very meaning of the word. According to Russell, the emotional content of the word 'good' accompanies its meaning, is a non-cognitive *part*, or perhaps *cohort*, of its meaning.

A Complete Theory

Ultimately, the strength of Russell's enlightened emotivism rests in its synthesis with his work on desire and impulse. As an ethical theory, emotivism is overwhelmingly psychological – it depends to a great degree on its analysis of relevant psychological concepts as they apply to moral beliefs, actions, judgments and general vocabulary. That this is so is not at all surprising, for emotivism's roots are in psychology. Yet Ayer and Stevenson make no attempt to present a convincing, comprehensive or even cursory analysis of the psychological terms and phenomena relevant to ethics, much less their relation to ethical activity. They took it for granted – and because of that, their theories are at best incomplete.

Russell, on the other hand, attempted to make sense of psychological concepts and phenomena in the early stages of his emotivism, and although he did not explicitly make use of this work in his enlightened emotivism, he quite likely took it for granted. Because his use of the terms was consistent with that early work, I expect he had clarified those issues to his satisfaction and then moved on. By explicitly combining the insights found in *The Analysis of Mind* and *Principles of Social Reconstruction* with his enlightened emotivism, we find a theory more nuanced, subtler, and more sophisticated than the more popular varieties of emotivism.

More importantly, whether we are persuaded or not, we see that Russell has a complete theory – one which takes all relevant phenomena into account and attempts to explain them. That alone sets him apart. That he stumbles is regrettable. That he is superior to his fellow emotivists despite his stumbling is cause for celebration.

Before we celebrate, though, let us compare Russell's integrated emotivism point-by-point with its rivals by way of a final assessment.

Notes

1. See Russell, *Auto Two*, 20. At this stage, desire did not play a large role in his emotivism. But we find, in *Principles of Social Reconstruction*, the seeds of his later synthesis of 'desire to desire' theory and emotivism. His take on desire and impulse changed hardly at all from this point on.
2. Kennedy, 'Nourishing life', 169.
3. Bertrand Russell, *Principles of Social Reconstruction* (London: Unwin Books, 1916), 11; henceforth 'Russell, *PSR*'.
4. Ibid.
5. Ibid. 12.
6. Bertrand Russell, *The Analysis of Mind* (London: Routledge, 1921), 65; henceforth 'Russell, *AM*'. Wittgenstein, in his famous objection, appears to have ignored the conditions under which one behaviour-cycle can be interrupted, and even replaced, by another in the same person or in someone else.
7. Ibid., 63. Or if, one prefers, 'a lack or deficiency is filled'.
8. Ibid., 62.

9. Ibid., 76.
10. Ibid. Emphasis added.
11. The last clause may lead one to believe that what is desired is that everyone work for peace. However, it is simply a description of the behaviour-cycle that those who say 'Peace is good' would enter in order to bring about quiescence. 'Working for peace is good' (in other words, 'Would that everyone worked for peace') would involve a different behaviour-cycle – one intended to *persuade others* to work for peace, perhaps. Obviously the two are not mutually exclusive; they would likely accompany one another.
12. To which he was likely driven in an attempt to avoid intentionality.
13. Ibid., 72.
14. Ibid.
15. Ibid.
16. Ibid., 73. Emphasis added.
17. Note the similarity to James here. Although Russell and James quarrelled over many points, they appear to have had more in common than either would admit (though Russell, for instance, did profess admiration for James' *Principles of Psychology* and was inclined to accept a qualified form of James' definition of truth as a set of criteria, though not a definition).
18. Russell, *AM*, 74.
19. Given how important the concept of impulse was to him during the First World War period, its omission from *Religion and Science, What I Believe* and *Power* is difficult to comprehend.
20. Russell, *AM*, 59. Clearly, in their paradigmatic forms, behaviourism and psychoanalysis are wholly incompatible – they sit at opposite extremes of the internalist/externalist spectrum. Russell's versions of both are idiosyncratic.
21. Russell, *PSR*, 31. Throughout this chapter, I will treat 'impulse' and 'instinct', as used by Russell, synonymously. He appears to assume they *are* synonyms, and although this may lead to minor problems at some point, I am not concerned with them here.
22. Ibid., 14. Although many people may desire or need work in itself, I do not find it plausible that most of the paid work that occupies their time is that which they would desire in itself. Nor does Russell, who deals with this matter at length in *The Conquest of Happiness*.
23. Russell, *PSR*, 12
24. Ibid.
25. Ibid.

26.   Ibid., 13.
27.   Ibid., 13–14.
28.   Ibid., 161.
29.   Bertrand Russell, *The Scientific Outlook*, 2nd edition (London: Routledge, 1949), 218–9.
30.   Russell, *PSR*, 162.
31.   Ibid.
32.   Ibid., 19.
33.   Ibid.
34.   Ibid.
35.   In the latter case, he sometimes advocates external (institutional) controls as well.
36.   A desire for happiness and peace is also incompossible with a desire for cruelty and suffering. Yet since the latter is not universalizable – and is, in fact, incompossible with many other universalizable desires – the desire for happiness and peace's incompossibility with the desire for cruelty and suffering would not matter to Russell.
37.   See Russell, *RS*, 231.
38.   Then again, they do not conflict with the self-interests of those banes of every ethical theory: sado-masochistic psychopaths. We do not have space to discuss such people here. Since they wreak havoc with *every* ethical theory that I have come across, I am not inclined to treat the consequences of their existence as an objection against Russell in particular. Personally, I am as inclined to exclude sado-masochistic psychopaths from ethical consideration as I am non-human animals, except insofar as they are *objects* of ethically-relevant behaviour.
39.   Russell, *PSR*, 163.
40.   Ibid., 26.
41.   Ibid., 27.
42.   In Russell's analysis, an intrinsic good is an object of universalizable desire.
43.   Ibid., 29.
44.   As his behaviourism progressed, Russell may have eliminated the principle of growth altogether, reinterpreting the principle's activity in terms of behaviour-cycles leading to the creation and realization of potential.
45.   He does not believe that suppressing desires is quite as dangerous, presumably because they are less fundamental, less integral to our natures (our 'instinctive' aspects), and since they are a couple of steps removed from the principle of growth. With desires, too, the

matter appears to be less one of suppression and more one of control and decision.

46. Thanks again to Nick Griffin for this one.
47. Russell, *AM*, 59. I have, obviously, paraphrased and altered Russell's example to make it more interesting for myself.
48. If her own sense of self-worth is threatened by Albert's activity – perhaps she feels ashamed that she does nothing to help anyone – self-interest will also lead her to interpret his actions in a manner that will make her seem morally superior to him.
49. Ibid., 60–1.
50. Ibid., 61.
51. Russell, *PSR*, 14–15.
52. He might not have contradicted himself if he meant only that some impulsive activities promote life and growth and love, etc.
53. 'Would that everyone desired excitement!' and 'Would that everyone desired pleasure!' are both universalizable. For more on how Russell conceives of desire and pleasure, and his recognized 'goods', see *The Conquest of Happiness*.
54. Russell, *PSR*, 17.
55. Ibid., 15.
56. Ibid.
57. Ibid., 29.
58. Ibid., 164.
59. Ibid.
60. Ibid.
61. Ibid., 165.
62. Aiken, *BRPM*, 95. Approval here means that the speaker would call X 'good'.
63. Russell, *PSR*, 163.
64. Ibid., 11.
65. Ibid. Emphasis added.
66. Aiken, *BRPM*, 85. Aiken also writes that, unlike Hume, Russell believes reason is a necessary component of the good life. I am not sure that he does. Intelligence and knowledge, certainly. Reason, perhaps, as the only reliable *means* to knowledge.
67. Bertrand Russell, 'Reason: The slave of the passions,' Pigden, *RoE*, 170.
68. Ibid.
69. Russell, *OP*, 187.
70. Aiken, *BRPM*, 87.

71.   Ibid.
72.   Ibid., 88.

5

Final Thoughts

The Story So Far

Let's recap.

We found the emotivist theories of Ayer and Stevenson, along with Russell's early attempt, inadequate for several reasons. Ayer's theory fails from the start because it depends on the verification principle, which cannot meet its own test. Even if we were to ignore that defect, Ayer's and Stevenson's theories fail because of their circularity. Since they do not provide standards for ethical reasoning, their theories cannot be applied reliably to moral decision-making and make moral criticism impossible. Furthermore, they assume without explanation that ethics is necessarily self-referential, when it seems obvious that ethics is only *sometimes* self-referential. Finally, Ayer and Stevenson abstract ethics so far from humanity that it loses much of its meaning and purpose. This last problem, combined with the previous two, suggest that Ayer and Stevenson missed the point of ethics altogether. They concentrated exclusively on the meaning of ethical terms and judgments, forgetting why we use them.

Seriously criticizing Russell's early theory is a difficult task – for he does not seem to have provided us with a theory at all. Even collecting the fragments he gives us during this period and using them to construct a theory is somewhat pointless, for we cannot be certain about exactly what he takes 'X is good' to mean, though his view *appears* to be similar in some respects to those of Ayer and Stevenson. His 'proto-emotivism' may not fall prey to the circularity objection (or it may, depending on how one interprets him), and unlike Ayer's it does not depend on the verification principle; but he too assumes that ethics is necessarily self-referential just because it is sometimes so. However, Russell remembered the point of ethics and spent far more time trying to explain the application of his ideas than he spent clarifying what he meant. A balance between the two would have been more helpful.

We have also examined Russell's enlightened emotivism. Aside from being an actual *theory*, this mature form of emotivism was superior to the others in several respects. Its use of universalizable impersonal desire enabled Russell to mix objective elements into a subjective theory, and combined with his theories of desire and impulse, enabled him to explain more moral phenomena than had its predecessors and avoid many of the criticisms levelled against them. Most importantly, it was designed to be practical, a useful aid to moral decision-making that contained standards for moral decision-making.

Regarding specific criticisms, Russell's theory is superior to the others simply because it is immune to some criticisms levelled against them. In proposing that 'X is good' means 'Would that everyone desired X', Russell avoids charges of circularity. Second, his enlightened emotivism makes extensive use of human concerns, needs and well-being – this is especially obvious when we incorporate his theories of desire and impulse. The agent, the human being who acts and is acted upon, is central to his project. As a consequence of its peculiar mixture of objective and subjective elements, Russell's mature theory manages to be simultaneously abstract and concrete. That same mixture may allow him to avoid Toulmin's criticism regarding ethical self-referentiality, since in the mature theory ethics includes both self-referential and 'objective' or 'external' elements. Finally, Russell's enlightened emotivism includes standards and criteria for ethical judgments and decision-making, indicating that he took the practical nature of ethics seriously.

Yet we found that even Russell's enlightened emotivism failed. First, it lacks any power to compel, any 'element of command'. It may be true that all moral theories lack this power, but that does not excuse Russell from making the attempt either to provide it or to explain why such a power is unnecessary, since the natural assumption is that it is. The fact that his theory lacks an element of command does not, I believe, make his theory worse than any other. Yet it does not set it above the pack either, and it is his responsibility to persuade us to accept it. Second, Pigden, following Geach, may have demonstrated that Russell's theory is incomplete since it cannot make sense of at least some moral arguments. Third, Russell's theory appears to apply less to activities and more to their description or characterization. Since the same act in the same context could be either good or bad, depending on how it is *described*, Russell's theory may not be as useful in making moral decisions as he wishes to believe. A related problem is that Russell does not provide us with a means for determining which desire is motivating someone. Nor does he tell us how general a desire must be in order for his theory to apply. The level of generality (in addition to the description), may have a significant impact on the 'goodness' or 'badness' of a desire.

We discovered that Russell's theory could be enriched by explicitly integrating his theories of desire and impulse into his enlightened emotivism. But this raised new problems. Russell's strange conception of unconscious desires, and the way in which he distinguished them from conscious desires, is difficult to swallow – if not blatantly incorrect. He also runs into trouble by assuming that the principle of growth is an intrinsic good, though he *could* be interpreted as maintaining that growth itself is what is intrinsically good, or that the principle of growth is identical with love. Perhaps the most significant problem faced by Russell's theory of desire is his concept of behaviour-cycles. Though attractive at first, his commitment to a sort of behaviourism prevents him from giving us a reliable means of distinguishing one behaviour-cycle from another (using, say, intentionality). Since behaviour-cycles share actions, since they are intertwined in a kind of network or web, since we cannot be certain when a particular desire is sated, or which actions were part of the behaviour-cycle that ended with the achievement of that goal, we cannot know what is desired. Making the same behaviouristic assumptions as Russell, we were forced to conclude that there are no distinct behaviour-cycles. Finally, there also seems to be a confusion of desire with impulse – it can be difficult, at times, to know which motivates a given activity. Russell gives us no way to distinguish between desire and impulse, though such a distinction is quite relevant to ethical matters; desires, for example, drive moral judgments whereas impulses apparently do not. The lack of any reliable means for making this distinction and for distinguishing among behaviour-cycles prevents Russell's theory from being used as a reliable guide to ethical decision-making – and, perhaps, moral criticism. Our attempt to reinterpret and alter Russell's theory allowed us to set some problems aside, but not all.

We come now, unceremoniously, to the end of our journey, having attempted to fuse Russell's theories of desire and impulse with his enlightened emotivism, having considered countless arguments, criticisms, claims and objections along the way. Does our synthesis provide us with the means to deal with outstanding objections against Russel's mature emotivist theory? Thankfully, there were only a few worth taking seriously.

Dropping Behaviourism

Recall the Robin Hood scenario. We could say that one who steals small amounts from the rich to give to the poor is motivated by an impulse to help the less fortunate, and has a corresponding desire, say, to improve their lot. If we characterize the matter in this way, we may say that Robin Hood is acting morally. 'Would that everyone desired to improve the lot of the less fortunate' is universalizable, and is plausibly inspired by love (which we may understand as a creative impulse or perhaps even the principle of growth itself) and guided by knowledge.

However, we found that one could characterize Robin Hood's motivations in less benevolent terms. He may have a possessive impulse to steal and a corresponding desire for the property of others. The introduction of impulse into Russell's emotivism gives us more options, a larger stock of characterizations – but we still have no way to determine which is the 'correct' one. In addition, Russell's behaviourism prohibits us from seeking refuge in intentionality. We must ask: 'What is the termination point of the behaviour-cycle in question?' Say it is the acquisition of someone else's property. In that case, we could say Robin Hood has a desire to steal. If it terminates when he gives that property to the needy, we could say he has a desire to help the less fortunate (provided they are not prosecuted for receiving stolen goods!). Remember, though, that the task of distinguishing between behaviour-cycles, and between desires, and accurately determining their 'purposes' is all but impossible in some cases. So we still have no reliable way to determine the correct characterization of a desire.

And what of impulse? Russell's behaviourism prevents him from determining which impulses people have except by paying attention to their actions. But Albert and Bertha's dispute indicated that unless one shares another's impulse, one is likely to misinterpret it. So, if Robin Hood is motivated by an impulse to help the less fortunate, we will understand (and be able to correctly characterize) that impulse *if we share it.* Otherwise, we may believe he simply has an impulse to steal. The problem is that Russell gives us no way to determine whether we share Robin Hood's impulse or not – and consequently, whether we are correctly interpreting his motivation. His theory traps us in hopeless confusion.

The same problem prevents us from settling the issue of Albert and Barney versus the fundamentalist mob. Russell cannot avoid the problem by generalizing the desires and impulses of the fundamentalists and homosexuals into classes because he cannot know what their desires and impulses are. Until he can do that, he has nothing to generalize except his own imposed interpretations of their impulses and desires, which will be coloured by whether or not he shares those impulses and desires – which he has no way of knowing. And we do not know whether it is legitimate to generalize the relevant desires in this way.

These are, I believe, the most significant problems that Russell's integrated emotivism[1] faces – the characterization of desires and impulses, distinguishing among desires and impulses, and the various problems related to the inability of his theory to distinguish among different desires and impulses due to the nature of behaviour-cycles. The second and third problems stem, by and large, from his behaviouristic assumptions. Yet he could abandon the behaviourism without significantly altering his emotivism, and a few slight modifications in the foundational assumptions would make a world of difference. Although I cannot, of course, pursue alternatives to behaviourism in any great detail, I will briefly outline a possible course of action.

For instance, identifying desires by their goal or object in the mind of the desiring individual instead of by whatever brings about quiescence would greatly alleviate the problem of distinguishing between desires. Russell's definition of desire as a longing for that which one does not possess, or for a state of affairs that does not yet exist, could remain. In fact, identifying desires by what they are a longing *for* in the mind of the desiring agent strikes me as a far more natural fit with his definition of desire. Identifying them in this way will lead us to new problems, but I expect they are less serious than those which face behaviouristic identification.[2] Though it may be relatively simple to identify one's own conscious desires by what one perceives as their object, identifying the desires of others will be difficult, since we have no access to their minds and must trust their reports.

We could retain the concept of behaviour-cycles without behaviourism. A behaviour-cycle could be, simply, a series of actions intended to achieve a desired result. Russell wants to avoid talk of intentionality, but we have discovered that intentionality cannot be cut out of the picture. It intrudes naturally, perhaps necessarily. So let us say that behaviour-cycles continue until their desired result has been achieved, or perhaps until the agent believes it has been achieved. And we may still call the desired result the 'purpose' of the behaviour-cycle. The difference between this and Russell's behaviouristic explanation is that Russell allows (or is forced to allow) whatever brings quiescence to be taken as the 'purpose' of the behaviour-cycle, whereas we are proposing that the purpose of a behaviour-cycle is what it is *intended* to achieve. In many cases, I expect the difference between the two positions is negligible – it will not make any practical difference. Yet from a theoretical standpoint, I find it less cumbersome, and not as obviously problematic, to allow intentionality into the picture.

On the other hand, Russell appears to require that we infer an *impulse* from the fact that someone is engaging in a certain sort of activity. From the fact that someone is eating we may infer that she had an impulse to eat. Yet we found that it may be more accurate to speak of impulses and desires as paired at least some of the time, perhaps necessarily. And it may be that the person in question is eating not because of an impulse, but because of a desire, say, for better health. Since impulses do not have any goals apart from the activity to which they lead, how do we know that impulse is operating at all? It does not terminate at the achievement of any goal, since it does not really have any goals. When we encounter behaviour, how do we know whether it is part of a behaviour-cycle (or cycles) intended to lead to the satisfaction of a desire, or that it is an end in itself, motivated by an impulse? Internally, we may reflect that we are not, say, eating because we feel a longing for food (that is, a desire), only that we want to eat. So it may be possible to distinguish between desires and impulses internally, at least some of the time. When it comes to other people, though, we have nothing. At best we could try to make an analogy between their behaviour and ours. Coming across a stranger eating, we could compare her activity with remembrances of our own, perhaps reflecting that when we eat we do so sometimes from impulse, sometimes from desire, sometimes both. Under what circumstances have we engaged in the behaviour-cycle of eating from desire? We may have eaten certain kinds of food out of a desire to lose weight or generally improve health. Now we could take notice of what this person is eating. If it is a heaped plate of fries and gravy with a side of buttered beef, desires for better health and weight loss are unlikely to have anything to do with the activity. So we could conclude then, reasonably, that the person is eating from impulse. Or from an impulse to eat combined with a desire for sheer gustatory pleasure!

The whole process is complicated. The point, though, is that we can infer from the behaviour of others, using comparisons with our own remembered behaviour and desires, whether impulse or desire is operative – and if so, which one and which kind. We may never be certain, but we can draw reasonable inferences.

Returning to our attempt to rid Russell's emotivism of all

traces of behaviourism, we should note that doing so robs Wittgenstein's objection of any power it might have had, since we are no longer identifying desires by the termination point of behaviour-cycles. By identifying desires in terms of their object, we make the task of distinguishing among them much easier as well. It does not matter that the same actions may be shared by multiple behaviour-cycles: the desire is distinguished at the beginning of the cycle, in the mind. And no longer do we need to wait for a behaviour-cycle's completion to know which desire is driving it. In these respects, ridding Russell's integrated emotivism of behaviouristic traces prevents significant problems from arising.

The fact that there are no absolutely distinct behaviour-cycles also becomes less problematic than it was for Russell's behaviouristic theory. We may accept that every behaviour-cycle overlaps with many others, that at any given time we are in the midst of several different behaviour-cycles motivated by several different desires and impulses, that identical series of actions may be part of several behaviour-cycles at once, and that much of the time we cannot tell when a behaviour-cycle has ended. None of these facts presents a problem for Russell's metaethic once its behaviouristic aspects have been flushed out, since desires are distinguished internally.

Although it seems clear that ridding Russell's emotivism of all behaviouristic traces makes it much more plausible, it does not solve every problem. Most importantly, it does not help us understand how to characterize actions accurately. We saw the consequences of Russell's lack of standards for this task in the examples of Robin Hood, and the fundamentalist mob versus Albert and Barney. When Russell claims that we cannot understand the desires and impulses of another unless we share or have shared them, he makes a plausible point. And it may be that we cannot begin to understand anyone else's desires and impulses except through a somewhat complex series of analogies and inferences, the veracity of which will be continually in doubt.

Russell's failure to provide standards for the correct characterization of desires and impulses is a serious defect nonetheless – one that has an enormous impact on the ability of his theory to provide a basis for moral criticism and decision-making. Perhaps someone could step in and add such standards to the theory on Russell's behalf. I expect the result would be worth the effort.

The Importance of Impulse

The addition of impulse to Russell's enlightened emotivism at a more fundamental level would also clear up a lot of problems. Given how important impulse is to much of his other work, Russell's exclusion of it from his formal ethics is rather odd, and his theory could have been stronger had he given it a prominent role. For instance, he could have defined 'good' in terms of both desire and impulse – perhaps even impulse alone. 'Peace is good' could mean: 'Would that everyone desired peace and had an impulse to engage in peace-making activity'.

In fact, impulse, recall, is more fundamental to moral activity than desire. It motivates instinctive activity and gives rise to desires. It comes naturally, not after soul-searching deliberation. Most importantly, if one can be educated into possessing the 'right' creative impulses, one will feel and desire compossible desires. A person whose impulses were 'virtuous' would be *automatically* virtuous, engaging in moral activity unthinkingly, acting out of love without hesitation. We have quoted Russell's claim that the best people have been those who had a broad range of impersonal desires, which stem from a nature filled with limitless sympathy – which I would identify with *the impulse to love others*, or *instinctive liking.*

The only problem I can see with this Russellian superhero[3] is that he might be unable to adapt effectively to novel situations, not being the sort who takes consequences into account on a situational basis. A being of impulse acts instinctively, consequences be damned. No matter how virtuous he might be, no matter how vast his knowledge, no matter how much he loves every little hair on every person's head, there may be situations in which acting unthinkingly on a creative impulse will lead to disaster. The superhero would be morally inadequate for the same reason rule-based ethical systems are inadequate: life is unpredictable. Furthermore, unless the rest of the world is similarly inclined, the Russellian superhero would be a perpetual victim. A being of love and generosity and benevolence who does not adjust his behaviour according to the probable consequences of his actions would be an easy target for those predatory folk bursting with possessive impulses. If asked for his belongings, would he not give them? If told to do something, would he not do it? What in his nature would prevent him from being a slave? Creative impulses, like sensible rules, might be adequate in many, perhaps most, situations. But something more is needed to deal with novel circumstances. In fact, in a world such as ours, a balance of creative *and* possessive impulses may be necessary – or at least *some* possessive impulses may be necessary. But perhaps I am oversimplifying Russell's ideal.

Could Russell define the good in terms of impulses we may universally desire to have? For instance, could one say, 'Helping others is good', meaning, 'Would that everyone had an impulse to help others'? Most of the creative impulses, maybe all, could be called good, since they are by nature compossible with one another and capable of being universally desired.[4] He would probably need to drop the first of his criteria for the good life ('inspired by love'), though, since it appears to be an impulse itself, and replace it with 'inspired by the principle of growth'.

Unless, once again, we can identify the principle of growth with love.

The Consequences of Objectivity

Those disturbed by subjectivist theories of ethics may take comfort in the fact that Russell's emotivism contains a great deal of objectivity and naturalism – more than he realized. If the Good is, roughly, that which we can reasonably imagine is desirable by everyone, then whether or not something is good is a matter of fact. Either X is desirable by everyone or it is not. Whether or not two desires are compossible is another matter of fact. Each of these is a naturalistic matter, and answers to the questions one might turn them into have truth-values. In fact, the objective/naturalistic elements of Russell's theory far out-number the subjective elements – further distancing him from the more famous emotivists, who were overwhelmingly sub-jectivistic. Even when Russell is outlining his theory, claiming that the Good is that which everyone desires, we must ask whe-ther there is anything that everyone desires – and if so, what. Again, either there is or is not something that everyone desires. And the answer to what it is that everyone desires will have a truth-value as well. All of this is naturalistic.

The most significant consequence of the great number of naturalistic and objective elements in a subjective theory is that it makes the theory far more appealing than its rivals. Those of us who are disturbed by ethical subjectivity are more likely to take seriously a form of emotivism in which, amidst a wealth of factual claims, the only significant subjective element is the optative nature of moral judgments.

But one of those facts may cause some trouble. What is *actually* universally desired? Russell seems to believe, most of the time, that human beings are naturally selfish, horrible, bloodthirsty brutes. Given that nature, which desires are they likely to share? Again, the answer to this appears to turn on how we characterize desires, and to what degree of generality we are supposed to apply the test of universalizability. 'Would that everyone desired to hunt each other as lions hunt zebras' may not be universalizable. But 'Would that everyone desired to kill the wicked' might, since very few people actually consider themselves or their loved ones 'wicked' – and the desire expressed is compossible with other apparently universal desires, such as that for vengeance (justice), excitement, and the like.

The consequentialist element thus leads Russell into some of the same traps that catch utilitarians. As long as a desire like 'Would that everyone desired to kill the wicked' or 'Would that the wicked were removed from the Earth' is compossible with the desires of most people, is inspired by love and guided by knowledge, it's acceptable. The minority who are deemed wicked, then killed in the name of 'protecting the children' or some other such nonsense, will suffer. The desire to kill the wicked is certainly not compatible with their own desires. But it may be compatible with the desires of most people.

Recall Albert and Barney versus the fundamentalist mob. The mob could easily claim that its desires were not only universalizable (depending on characterization and level of generality), but inspired by love (their concern for the immortal souls of homosexuals) and guided by knowledge (of Paul's claims against homosexuals). Hitler was motivated, at least in part, by his love of Germany and his presumed 'knowledge' that certain kinds of people were wicked and injurious to the greater good, as he understood it. Here we have yet another problem caused by the lack of standards and criteria for characterization, interpretation, application and so forth. Although Russell's ideas and principles *may* be wonderful, we need to know how to use them properly if we are to prevent them from being used to call nearly anything good.

Furthermore, Russell may not have accomplished one of his own goals. Recall his conviction (after Santayana) that a belief in objective moral values leads to persecution and cruelty. Yet the universalizability of ethical judgments makes them objective in his theory. So would his theory not also lead to cruelty and persecution? Perhaps not the theory itself, once it has been qualified to rule out such abuses as those just discussed. He may need to require that knowledge of the degrees of subjectivity and objectivity in ethics be withheld for the general public, available only to a select group of ethicists. The public may need to be persuaded (manipulated) into believing that ethics is entirely subjective, so that they don't move toward cruel dogma. In this case, ethicists would be acting in the role of the Preacher, that role so dear to Russell. The consequences of manipulating the public into false beliefs about ethics may be better than the consequences of telling them the truth. I find this disturbing, though it seems clear that if one makes the same assumptions as our three emotivists, nothing conclusive can be said against it. The mistake may lie in the assumption that a belief in objective values leads *necessarily* to cruelty and persecution. It often does; that much history makes clear. But it need not be that way. Perhaps once ethics has finally been divorced from religion *completely*, in the public mind, such a consequence will become less common. Russell may have been led into this line of thought by the popular belief that objective ethics belongs in the sphere of religion.

Conclusion

It seems that we must end on a rather depressing note. Russell failed. He managed only to be a one-eyed man in the land of the blind, a king among emotivists – perhaps not among moral philosophers as a whole.

Late in life, Russell admitted that he was dissatisfied with his moral philosophy. 'I cannot see how to refute the arguments for the subjectivity of ethical values,' he lamented, 'but I find myself incapable of believing that all that is wrong with wanton cruelty is that I don't like it.'[5] He hoped, to the end, that someone would come along with a better theory to persuade him. Indeed, Russell believed that proving that wanton cruelty is bad was the test of a successful ethical theory.[6] Perhaps he was being too hard on himself, a side effect of the demanding intellectual conscience that guided so much of his work, sometimes against his will. I agree with Russell in feeling dissatisfied, and unconvinced, by his emotivist metaethic. However, as there is much of value in it as well, it cannot be summarily dismissed.

Russell managed to call attention to a host of features ignored or downplayed by other moral philosophers – the role of emotion and desire in ethics, for instance, was given only cursory attention by most philosophers. Some, such as Hume, tried to call attention to their importance, but were treated as sideshows. Russell and the other emotivists placed emotion and desire in positions of prominence. Emotivism's brief moment in the sun seems to have had a lasting effect: more philosophers are paying attention to the non-rational components of ethics. Russell's marriage of objectivity and subjectivity is also a marvel, one that should be extracted for use by other philosophers. And I believe that the synthesis of his enlightened emotivism with his theories of desire and impulse provide, at the very *least*, a fascinating object of study – and at *most*, something to be salvaged.

What I wish to see is an attempt to combine Russell's integrated emotivism with his normative ethics in a manner that takes into account advances since Russell's time – such as the defeat of behaviourism. This can be done, I think, and might even result in a convincing ethical theory. If nothing else, it would be fascinating to see how far an apologist could take Russell's ideas.

Even if his theory fails in the end, let us not lose sight of the fact that Russell was almost unique among philosophers in that he didn't merely attempt to understand ethics; he also attempted to engage with the world, to make a difference outside the ivy-covered walls of the university. His moral philosophy was intended to inform his moral practice, his activism, not merely languish in a dusty library. There is something admirable in that: whereas most philosophers *talk* about how we ought to think and act, what sets Russell apart is that he was one of only a handful of philosophers who used philosophy to inform an active engagement with the world. Russell put philosophy into practice – even though others couldn't understand why:

> During the last war, the War Office sent for me and exhorted me to preserve a sense of humour. With great difficulty I refrained from saying that the casualty lists made me split my sides with laughter. No, I will not be serene and above the battle; what is horrible I will see as horrible, and not as part of some blandly beneficent whole.[7]

Notes

1. By 'integrated emotivism' I mean Russell's enlightened emotivism combined with his theories of desire and impulse.
2. One problem for Russell the behaviourist is that he continually refers to phenomena that do not seem to be capable of purely behaviouristic explanation, such as unconscious desires and the blatant resort to intentionality in his distinction of possessive versus creative impulses. His recognition of this fact might explain his bizarre definition of unconscious desires and all the attendant behaviouristic trappings he wishes to attach to them.
3. When I refer to this ideal person as a 'Russellian superhero', I mean he or she is the ideal extrapolated from Russell's moral philosophy. Russell himself might have had a different ideal.

4. Note, though, that we would need to have a clear idea of precisely how impulses could be created and changed, since (for Russell and all other consequentialists) the right follows from the Good.

5. Bertrand Russell, 'Notes on "Philosophy"', *Collected Papers, Volume 11*, 310–1.

6. See Kenneth Blackwell, *The Spinozistic Ethics of Bertrand Russell* (London: George Allen & Unwin, 1985), 6.

7. Russell, Reply, 52.

BIBLIOGRAPHY

Aiken, Lillian W. *Bertrand Russell's Philosophy of Morals*. New York: The Humanities Press Inc., 1963. (Abreviated as *BRPM*)

Ayer, Alfred Jules. *Language, Truth and Logic*. 2nd edition. New York: Dover Publications, Inc., 1946. (*LTL*)

Barnes, W.H.F. 'A suggestion about value'. *Readings in Ethical Theory*. 2nd edition. Eds, Wilfrid Sellars and John Hospers. New York: Meredith Corporation, 1970. 241.

Blackwell, Kenneth. *The Spinozistic Ethics of Bertrand Russell*. London: George Allen & Unwin, Ltd, 1985.

Blanshard, Brand. 'The impasse in ethics – and a way out'. *Readings in Ethical Theory*. 2nd edition. Eds, Wilfrid Sellars and John Hospers. New York: Meredith Corporation, 1970. 288–301.

Brink, Andrew. *Bertrand Russell: The Psychobiography of a Moralist*. Atlantic Highlands: Humanities Press International, Inc., 1989.

Buchler, Justus. 'Russell and the principles of ethics'. *The Philosophy of Bertrand Russell*. 4th Edition. La Salle: Open Court, 1971. 511–35.

Clark, Ronald. *The Life of Bertrand Russell*. London: Jonathan Cape, Ltd, 1975.

Clarke, Peter. 'Bertrand Russell and the dimensions of edwardian liberalism'. *Intellect and Social Conscience*. Eds, Margaret Moran and Carl Spadoni. Hamilton: McMaster University Library Press, 1984. 207–21.

Denton, Peter H. *The ABC of Armageddon*. Albany: State University of New York Press, 2001.

Geach, P.T. *Logic Matters*. Oxford: Blackwell, 1972.

Goldman, Alan H. *Moral Knowledge*. London: Routledge, 1988.

Grayling, A.C. *Russell*. Oxford: Oxford University Press, 1996.

Griffin, Nick. Ed. *The Selected Letters of Bertrand Russell: The Private Years, 1884–1914*. Paperback edition. London: Routledge, 2002.

—— *The Selected Letters of Bertrand Russell: The Public Years, 1914–1970*. London: Routledge, 2001.

Feinberg, Barry and Ronald Kasrils. *Bertrand Russell's America: Volume One, 1896–1945*. London: George Allen & Unwin, Ltd, 1973.

Harrison, Brian. 'Bertrand Russell: The false consciousness of a feminist'. *Intellect and Social Conscience*. Eds, Margaret Moran and Carl Spadoni. Hamilton: McMaster University Library Press, 1984. 157–205.

Jager, Ronald. *The Development of Bertrand Russell's Philosophy*. London: George Allen & Unwin Ltd, 1972.

Kennedy, Thomas C. 'Nourishing life: Russell and the twentieth-century British peace movement, 1900–18'. *Intellect and Social Conscience*. Eds, Margaret Moran and Carl Spadoni. Hamilton: McMaster University Library Press, 1984. 223–36.

Kurtz, Paul Grimley. *Bertrand Russell*. Boston: Twayne Publishers, 1986.

Lewis, John. *Bertrand Russell: Philosopher and Humanist*. New York: International Publishers, 1968.

Monk, Ray. *Bertrand Russell: The Spirit of Solitude*. London: Vintage/Random House, 1997.

——*Bertrand Russell: The Ghost of Madness*. London: Jonathan Cape/Random House, 2000.

Monro, D.H. 'Russell's moral theories'. *Bertrand Russell: Critical Assessments*. Volume IV. Ed. A.D. Irvine. London: Routledge, 1999. 65–85.

Moore, G.E. *Principia Ethica*. Paperback edition. Cambridge: Cambridge University Press, 1962.

Nowell-Smith, P.H. *Ethics*. Middlesex: Penguin Books, 1954.

Odell, S. Jack. *On Russell.* Belmont: Wadsworth/Thomson Learning, 2000.

Pigden, Charles. *Russell on Ethics.* London: Routledge, 1999. (*RoE*)

—— 'Bertrand Russell: Moral philosopher or unphilosophical moralist?' *The Cambridge Companion to Bertrand Russell.* Ed. Nicholas Griffin. Cambridge: Cambridge University Press, 2003. 475–506. (BR)

Ross, Sir David. 'Critique of Ayer'. *Readings in Ethical Theory.* 2nd edition. Eds, Wilfrid Sellars and John Hospers. New York: Meredith Corporation, 1970. 250–1.

Ruja, Harry. 'Russell on the meaning of "good"'. *Intellect and Social Conscience.* Eds, Margaret Moran and Carl Spadoni. Hamilton: McMaster University Library Press, 1984. 137–56.

Russell, Bertrand. *The Analysis of Mind.* London: Routledge, 1921. (*AM*)

—— *The Autobiography of Bertrand Russell: Volume One, 1872–1914.* London: McClelland and Stewart Limited, 1967.

—— *The Autobiography of Bertrand Russell: Volume Two, 1914–1944.* London: McClelland and Stewart Limited, 1968. (*Auto Two*)

—— *The Autobiography of Bertrand Russell: Volume Three, 1944–1969.* New York: Simon and Schuster, 1969.

—— 'Behaviourism and values'. *Sceptical Essays.* London: George Allen & Unwin Ltd, 1928. 89–98.

—— *The Conquest of Happiness.* London: Horace Liveright, Inc., 1930.

—— *Education and the Social Order.* London: Routledge, 1932.

—— 'The elements of ethics'. *Philosophical Essays.* New York: Simon and Schuster, 1966. 13–59.

—— 'The ethics of war'. *Justice in Wartime.* 2nd edition. London: George R. Allen & Unwin, Ltd, 1917.

—— 'The expanding mental universe'. *The Basic Writings of Bertrand Russell, 1903–1959.* Eds, Robert E. Egner and Lester E. Denonn. New York: Simon and Schuster, 1961. 391–8.

—— 'A free man's worship'. *Mysticism and Logic*. 3rd edition. London: Unwin Books, 1963. 40–7.

—— 'Free thought and official propaganda'. *Sceptical Essays*. London: George Allen & Unwin Ltd, 1928. 146–83.

—— 'Freedom versus authority in education'. *Sceptical Essays*. London: George Allen & Unwin Ltd, 1928. 184–201.

—— *The Impact of Science on Society*. London: Unwin Hyman, 1952.

—— 'Individual and social ethics'. *The Basic Writings of Bertrand Russell, 1903–1959*. Eds, Robert E. Egner and Lester E. Denonn. New York: Simon and Schuster: New York, 1961. 357–66.

—— 'Light versus heat [1954]'. *The Collected Papers of Bertrand Russell, Volume 11*. Ed. John G. Slater. London: Routledge, 1997. 173–5.

—— *My Philosophical Development*. Revised edition. London: Routledge, 1995.

—— 'Mysticism and logic'. *Mysticism and Logic*. 3rd edition. London: Unwin Books, 1963. 9–30.

—— 'North Staffs' praise of war'. *Yours Faithfully, Bertrand Russell*. Ed. Ray Perkins, Jr. Illinois: Carus Publishing Company, 2002.

—— 'Notes on 'Philosophy'. *The Collected Papers of Bertrand Russell, Volume 11*. Ed. John G. Slater. London: Routledge, 1997. 310–1.

—— 'On denoting'. *Logic and Knowledge: Essays, 1901–1950*. Ed. Robert C. Marsh. London: George Allen & Unwin, Ltd, 1956. 39–56.

—— 'On the value of scepticism'. *Sceptical Essays*. London: George Allen & Unwin Ltd, 1928. 11–25.

—— *An Outline of Philosophy*. Revised edition. London: Routledge, 1995. (*OP*)

—— 'The place of science in a liberal education'. *Mysticism and Logic*. 3rd edition. London: Unwin Books, 1963. 31–9.

—— *Power: A New Social Analysis.* London: Routledge, 1938. (*Power*)

—— *Principles of Social Reconstruction.* London: Unwin Books, 1916. (*PSR*)

—— *Religion and Science.* Oxford: Oxford University Press, 1935. (*RS*)

—— 'Reply to criticisms'. *The Collected Papers of Bertrand Russell, Volume 11.* Ed. John G. Slater. London: Routledge, 1997. 18–64. (Reply)

—— 'Review of A.J. Ayer, Language, Truth, and Logic [1947]'. *The Collected Papers of Bertrand Russell, Volume 11.* Ed. John G. Slater. London: Routledge, 1997. 171–3.

—— *Roads to Freedom.* 3rd edition. London: Routledge, 1920.

—— 'On scientific method in philosophy'. *Mysticism and Logic.* 3rd edition. London: Unwin Books, 1963. 75–93.

—— *The Scientific Outlook.* 2nd edition. London: Routledge, 1949.

—— 'Styles in ethics'. *The Basic Writings of Bertrand Russell, 1903–1959.* Eds, Robert E. Egner and Lester E. Denonn. New York: Simon and Schuster, 1961. 345–50.

—— 'War and non-resistance'. *Russell on Ethics.* Ed. Charles Pigden. London: Routledge, 1999. 11–3.

—— 'What I believe'. *Why I Am Not a Christian.* Ed. Paul Edwards. New York: Simon and Schuster, 1957. 48–87. (WIB)

Ryan, Alan. *Bertrand Russell: A Political Life.* London: The Penguin Press, 1988.

Santayana, George. *Winds of Doctrine.* 2nd edition. New York: Charles Scribner's Sons, 1926.

Satris, Stephen. *Ethical Emotivism.* Dordrecht: Martinus Nijhoff Publishers, 1987.

Slater, John G. *Bertrand Russell.* Bristol: Thoemmes Press, 1994.

Stevenson, C.L. 'The emotive conception of ethics and its cognitive implications'. *Readings in Ethical Theory.* 2nd edition.

Eds, Wilfrid Sellars and John Hospers. New York: Meredith Corporation, 1970. 267–75.

—— 'The emotive meaning of ethical terms'. *Readings in Ethical Theory.* 2nd edition. Eds, Wilfrid Sellars and John Hospers. New York: Meredith Corporation, 1970. 254–66. (EMET)

—— *Ethics and Language.* New Haven: Yale University Press, 1944.

—— *Facts and Values: Studies in Ethical Analysis.* New Haven: Yale University Press, 1963.

Tait, Katharine. *My Father Bertrand Russell.* New York: Harcourt Brace Jovanovich, 1975.

Toulmin, Stephen. *An Examination of the Place of Reason in Ethics.* Cambridge: Cambridge University Press, 1950.

Warnock, Mary. *Ethics Since 1900.* 2nd edition. London: Oxford University Press, 1966.

Wellman, Carl. 'Emotivism and ethical objectivity'. *Readings in Ethical Theory.* 2nd edition. Eds, Wilfrid Sellars and John Hospers. New York: Meredith Corporation, 1970. 276–87.

Willis, Kirk. 'Introduction' to Bertrand Russell. *Power.* London: Routledge, 1938. vi–xiii.

Wollheim, Richard. 'Bertrand Russell and the liberal tradition'. *Bertrand Russell: Critical Assessments.* Volume IV. Ed. A.D. Irvine. London: Routledge, 1999. 98–109.

Wood, Alan. *Bertrand Russell: The Passionate Sceptic.* London: George Allen & Unwin Ltd, 1957.

Index

absolutism, moral 3, 4, 5, 10, 101, 110, 112 (*see also* objectivity, ethical)

activism 2, 10, 67, 106–8, 116–17, 174

attitude
ethical 23–6, 27–8, 31, 32, 34–7, 38–43, 46, 48–50, 55, 61, 62, 64, 67, 89, 91
logical opposition of 40, 42
religious 8

Ayer, Alfred Jules 1, 18, 19–20, 22, 23–4, 25, 26–7, 29, 34, 35–41, 43–4, 50, 51, 52, 53, 54–6, 62, 63, 68, 70–4, 82, 97, 100, 103, 107, 108, 110, 116, 153, 159, 160 (*see also* erification principle)

behaviour-cycle 126–7, 130, 141–4, 162, 163–4, 165–6, 167

behaviourism 124–5, 131, 141, 143, 162, 163–4, 165 n. 2, 166–7

Blanshard, Brand 47–50, 70

compassion (*see* general interest)

compossibility 42, 68, 85–7, 95, 98, 99, 110, 111, 113, 115, 151, 168, 170

concepts, ethical 19, 19 n. 3, 26–7, 29, 30–1, 44–5, 51–2, 54, 57–8, 71, 92

conscience 89

consequentialism 68, 101, 105, 109, 112, 139, 140, 142, 171

contradiction, ethical (*see* disagreement, ethical)

dance, interpretive 68, 128

democratic fallacy 30

Denton, Trevor 68–9

desire 2, 4–5, 14, 35, 57, 61, 68–9, 72, 83–8, 93–8, 99, 100, 101–3, 109, 110–11, 113, 117, 118, 123–31, 132, 134, 135, 141–2, 143–4, 145–8, 149, 150, 151, 152, 153, 160, 161, 162, 163, 164–6, 167–8
conflicts of 83, 88, 93
conscious 126–8, 129, 130, 141, 143, 161, 165
definition of 124
immature 84–6
impersonal (*see* universalizability)
mature 84–7, 96
purpose of 124
ranking 85
secondary 126–8, 129, 141
unconscious 126, 127, 128, 130, 142, 161

'desire to desire' theory 3, 4–5, 59 n. 123, 82, 83

disagreement, ethical 21–2, 27, 29, 33–43, 59, 65–6, 70, 71, 73, 93, 99, 105–6, 144–8
in attitude 34–5, 41–3
in belief 34–5

dispute (*see* disagreement)

education 89, 96, 125, 148, 149, 150, 151, 168

enlightened emotivism 1, 2, 3, 72, 82–118, 124, 127, 130, 153–4, 160

error theory 9n. 22

ethical naturalism 22–3, 68, 170–2

First World War 2, 6, 10–14, 66, 82, 106, 123

●

freedom 138
fundamentalism, Christian 114–16, 164, 167, 171

Geach, P. T. 112
general interest 14, 35, 95, 102, 103, 111, 168
good
    connotations of 152–3
    definition of 21–3, 33, 50, 59–60, 68, 71, 92, 93, 169
    intrinsic 92–3, 138–9
good life 98, 109, 111, 114, 133, 136, 151, 169

hatred 12–13, 94–5, 145
Hobbes, Thomas 21–2
homosexuality 114–16, 164, 167, 171
human nature 13
Hume, David 22, 102, 151, 152

impulse 2, 14, 100, 117, 118, 124, 128, 130–7, 139, 140, 143–51, 153, 160, 161, 162, 163–4, 165–8
    creative 133, 135, 136–7, 140, 141, 151, 163, 168
    possessive 133–4, 135, 136–7, 140, 151, 163, 169
incompossibility (*see* compossibility)
instinct (*see* impulse)
interest theory 22, 22 n. 16, 23, 34 (*see also* simple subjectivism)
intuitionism 3, 3 n. 2, 3 n. 3, 4, 5, 6, 9, 10, 11–12, 13, 14, 18, 53, 56

judgment, ethical 10, 19, 20, 22, 24–9, 30, 34–7, 39, 43–4, 50–1, 53, 60, 61, 65, 68, 70, 71, 73, 83, 93, 95, 100, 102, 104, 105, 108, 109, 113, 117, 153, 159

Kant, Immanuel 94
kippers 42
knowledge, ethical 34, 41, 53, 69, 82–3

language
    ethical 1, 3, 9, 19–21, 23–38, 43–56, 59–60, 61, 63, 66, 70, 71, 83, 96–7, 99, 108, 153, 159, 160
    religious 8–9
legislator, way of the 88–90, 95
liking, instinctive 137–8, 168

meaning, emotive 31–3, 45, 47, 153
Moore, G. E. 3, 4–5, 6, 9, 23, 36, 40, 53, 56 (*see also* open question argument)
Morrell, Ottoline 6–8, 14

naturalistic fallacy 56

obedience 89–90
objectivity, ethical 4, 5, 6, 10, 11, 26, 28, 30, 44, 57, 58, 62, 68, 93, 94, 101, 103, 104, 107–8, 109–10, 111–12, 170–2, 173
obligation 101, 102
open question argument 23 (*see also* Moore, G. E.)

Pearsall-Smith, Alys 5, 7
Perry, R. B. 61–5
Pigden, Charles 39, 40, 45, 50, 71, 111, 112
preacher, way of the 63, 68, 88, 90–2, 172
principle of growth 134–5, 137, 138, 139 n. 44, 148–9, 151, 161–2, 163, 169–70
propaganda (*see* preacher, way of the)
properties, moral 3, 4, 9–10
proto-emotivism 1, 6, 18, 56–74, 159–60
psychoanalysis 124, 131
psychological egoism 69, 70, 92, 103, 117, 124–6, 142, 170–1
punishment 65

questions, ethical 20–1

reason 41, 50–1, 65, 67, 71–2, 87, 91, 98, 103–4, 105–6, 108, 132, 151–2
religion 7, 8, 82
  non-credal 8–9, 14
rhetoric (*see* preacher, way of)
Ross, Sir David 27–30, 39–40, 50, 70
Ruja, Harry 4–5

Santayana, George 4–5, 6, 8, 11, 14
science 82, 83, 92, 93, 98, 105
self-interest 55 (*see also* psychological egoism)
  enlightened 96
sentences, ethical (*see* language, ethical)
simple subjectivism 6, 18, 21–3, 26, 27, 36, 56–60, 59 n. 123, 71, 116 (*see also* 'desire to desire' theory, interest theory, and proto-emotivism)
Stevenson, Charles L. 1, 18, 20–6, 29, 30–5, 38, 40, 41–3, 44–7, 49–50, 51, 52, 53, 54–6, 63, 66, 68, 70–4, 82, 91, 97, 100, 102, 108, 110, 116, 123, 153, 159, 160
  descriptive use 24, 32, 45
  dynamic use 24, 30, 31–2
  substitution criterion 21
  three requirements 21–3

superhero, Russellian 168–9
sympathy (*see* general interest)

terms, ethical (*see* concepts, ethical and language, ethical)
theory of descriptions 4, 9, 9 n. 23, 14,
Toulmin, Stephen 50–6, 71, 110
truth, ethical 19, 23, 30, 35, 41, 45, 53, 55, 60, 70, 82, 94

universalizability 68, 69, 87, 89, 93–5, 98, 102, 105, 110, 111, 113, 114–16, 135–6, 139, 140, 151, 160, 163, 169, 170, 171

validity, ethical 45–7, 52–3, 55, 66, 99–100
  semantic 46
  syntactic 46–7
verification principle 19, 27, 43–4, 70, 100, 159

Wellman, Carl 41–3, 44–7, 50, 66, 70
Whitehead, Alfred North 7
will 124, 125, 134, 135, 148, 149, 150
Wittgenstein, Ludwig 141–2, 167
World War One (*see* First World War)